BEST CANADIAN ESSAYS

2020

EDITED BY

SARMISHTA SUBRAMANIAN

T0160393

BIBLIOASIS

WINDSOR, ONTARIO

FIRST EDITION
ISBN 978-1-77196-366-4 (Trade Paper)
ISBN 978-1-77196-367-1 (eBook)

Edited by Sarmishta Subramanian
Copyedited by Emily Donaldson
Cover and text designed by Gordon Robertson

Published with the generous assistance of the Canada Council for the Arts, which last year invested $153 million to bring the arts to Canadians throughout the country, and the financial support of the Government of Canada. Biblioasis also acknowledges the support of the Ontario Arts Council (OAC), an agency of the Government of Ontario, which last year funded 1,709 individual artists and 1,078 organizations in 204 communities across Ontario, for a total of $52.1 million, and the contribution of the Government of Ontario through the Ontario Book Publishing Tax Credit and Ontario Creates.

PRINTED AND BOUND IN CANADA

CONTENTS

Sarmishta Subramanian
Introduction   1

Michelle Orange
How Free Is Too Free?:
Surveillance Capitalism, Market Democracy,
and the Dangers of Modern Freedom   11

Carl Wilson
It's Too Late to Cancel Michael Jackson   21

Michael LaPointe
The Unbearable Smugness of Walking   29

Alexandra Kimball
The Loneliness of Infertility   35

Benjamin Leszcz
The Life-Changing Magic of Making Do   49

Larissa Diakiw
The Disneyland of Death   59

Andy Lamey
  In the US Campus Speech Wars,
  Palestinian Advocacy Is a Blind Spot   73

Wayne Grady
  Syncopes   89

Christina Sharpe
  Beauty Is a Method   103

Alexandra Molotkow
  Selfish Intimacy   109

Jeremy Narby
  Confessions of a White Vampire   115

James Brooke-Smith
  Meritocracy and Its Discontents   123

Jenny Ferguson
  Off Balance   135

Andrew Nikiforuk and Amorina Kingdon
  From Berth to Death   153

Alanna Mitchell
  For the Love of Pronghorns   167

Contributors' Biographies   177
Publications Consulted   181
Acknowledgements   183

INTRODUCTION

Sarmishta Subramanian

This book—like most that have found their way into the world this fall—began life in the Before Times. These essays were written in a long-ago 2019, and I read many of them, and others, in an also distant 2020 in a café with an elegant sofa, a cup of bergamot-scented tea on the table before me. Sometimes (glorious to think of now) I'd be annoyed by the music—dramatic French songs or bad contemporary pop that I would never listen to at home—or find myself distracted by a years-old *New Yorker* left on the table: the sort of accidental diversions we used to encounter in those times, a consequence of sharing spaces that were not our own with people we didn't know. The loss of novelty is not the point, but rather of unpredictability, the unknown, the uncontrollable, the unpatrolled.

Exactly the opposite impulses guide us today. At some point along this book's journey, the world changed. The moment can be marked precisely by a calendar date (March 12, the day symphony concerts and NBA and NHL games disappeared from calendars) or a Covid-19 case count (179 in this country, an innocent number, so modest it makes you gasp). In the world we now inhabit, any unpredictable element carries risk. So we have learned to weigh and debate acts that were once routine and spontaneous, courting daily what psychologists have dubbed decision fatigue. For long stretches of 2020, we have regarded the world, many of us, with the cold canniness of insurance adjusters or algorithms, calculating and recalculating risk and benefit. We are finely attuned to micro-fluctuations in each—well, except for those of us who aren't, who inadvertently re-up the risk-aversion quotient for the rest of us.

I read Wayne Grady's essay "Syncopes" in the Before Times. It begins with a fainting spell (the medical term is "syncope") the author had at the fantastically picturesque Shouldice hospital in Toronto, following hernia surgery. The syncopes he discusses are more often not medical; as a linguistic term, a syncope refers to an elided or disappeared sound in a word. In music it gives rise to syncopation, the disruption of an established rhythm with the addition of opposing new rhythms. Grady travels, figuratively speaking, from the floor of a lounge at the Shouldice, where he was found by nurses following his loss of consciousness, to consider the impact of other elisions and disappearances. He does so via Vladimir Nabokov; the journalist Masha Gessen's reflections on syncopes; the Second World War; his own father's journey as a biracial Black man. It's an erudite, meandering reflection on moments of displacement that change us.

By the spring, when I was re-reading these essays, Grady's rumination about the intersection of the medical, the literary, and the cultural, to form a kind of theory of loss and arrival had suddenly become an encapsulation of the present moment. Many of the world's citizens were experiencing something unusual: a kind of single global syncope, a shared loss, a stormy interruption to consciousness brought about by the same event. "A syncope," Grady writes, can be "either a significant absence or an accentuated presence." The universal syncope created by the coronavirus seemed to be both things at once. Its presence embodied absences: blank spots in our financial systems, our economies, our health care planning, our political systems, our foundational social structures. And it simultaneously made present things we'd forgotten to notice or whose worth we'd stopped seeing: the effort of producing food, which encompasses all of two percent of GDP, and matters more than most of the other ninety-eight; the inadequately compensated labour of caregiving—more work without which societies can hardly function; the nature and value of kinship.

That last issue, a big one, has become more legible in an era of lockdowns and social bubbles. The signs of disquiet are everywhere: the loneliness of grandparents stranded in empty houses or vertiginous condos; the harried lives of parents suddenly raising children unaided; those children, cut off from many of the nourishing connections in their lives. One theme that has emerged is the culpability of the nuclear family in all this isolation, though the flaws in that model were not entirely invisible in the past. Their effects were familiar to anyone answering the demands of aging parents and growing children and encroaching, ever-intensifying jobs. Who is served well by these discrete, self-sufficient units of community? Not elderly grandparents; not children; not, often enough, most of the individuals involved. Such is the allure of freedom; we choose it even when it constrains us. "How free is too free?" Michelle Orange asks in the essay that opens this collection. That question, she notes, "may have boggled democracies throughout history, but never in quite the way it now boggles ours." Orange is exploring the paradox of freedom in the context of surveillance capitalism and modern democracy, but it applies in other areas, including the reality of human connection.

In the West, it must be said, the nuclear family is not exactly a recent phenomenon, unless one considers the thirteenth century to be recent. The nuclear family apparently didn't elbow its way to the top helped along by industrialization, or late capitalism, or a neoliberal consensus; medieval English parish records show this was how people lived in those times, too. But alternative models, of close and interconnected communities, have long thrived in other places, and still do. I found myself, in lockdown in Toronto, envying my aunts and uncles and their children and grandchildren in Delhi, who live in five independent but interlocked households separated by a few hundred feet and two or three sets of stairs. They converse from balconies; in the lockdown's most stringent weeks they could run food and supplies back to each other. Almost no one enjoys the freedoms, or burdens, of living alone.

It's hard not to be keenly aware of that tradeoff in this time. After all, in the absence of office work, shopping, gym trips, yoga classes, travel, restaurants and the terrifically productive business of errand running that seems to take up so much of modern life, what remains but human connection— or its lack? Long before the pandemic, social isolation was a serious affliction in the West, enough to merit its own government ministry in the United Kingdom (for a time), and discussions of the same in Australia. Loneliness as a hazard to physical health has been the focus of research and study; a lack of human connection leaves a deeper imprint on lifespan than obesity or air pollution, and it is on an equal footing with diabetes in hastening mortality. The elderly in Western societies are especially vulnerable, experts warned for years, as are those with mental health issues.

For those who struggled before, the questions now are more dire. Vancouver has seen soaring cases of drug overdoses; and it cannot be coincidence that it was during the pandemic that Sarah Hegazi, the fearless Egyptian LGBT activist, haunted by three months of imprisonment and torture in her country before she fled to Canada, died by suicide. Separated from a close-knit family and friends back home, she'd spoken of the loneliness of exile. "Home is not land and borders. It's about people you love," she told the CBC in 2018, soon after she moved. "Here in Canada, I haven't people, I haven't family."

Hegazi's story is exceptional; that sentiment, among those who've left their home countries to settle in the West, is not. And in this time, when social isolation is in essence medically prescribed, the reach of loneliness has been more catholic. Surely many North Americans, relieved of the demands of community and extended family in the Before Times, happy enough to be bowling alone, must be pondering some questions: Who are the essential people in our lives? Do we accord them the time and care they deserve? Do we have enough of them?

Some definitions restrict kinship to marital bonds or blood relationships, but the American cultural anthropologist Marshall Sahlins saw kinship as "mutuality of being ... people who are intrinsic to one another's existence." The Western Tibetan word for friend translates rather poetically to "happiness-grief-identical," and Trukese communities in Micronesia use the term "my sibling from the same canoe." That's a wonderful metaphor that in Trukese lore is not so much a metaphor, describing rather the ties forged when individuals face together the perils of the sea. It is a reminder, too, of another tradeoff, between security and connection. Financial stability and robust state structures that keep societies safer may also weaken some of the mystical bonds that bind us. The countries in which the greatest numbers of people live alone are also some of the world's wealthiest. A less perilous sea, it seems, is also a lonelier one.

"Syncope ... refers to a thing that was there, has been forgotten, and then suddenly is there again," Grady writes in his piece. If the pandemic descended on us all, forcing profound questions about how we live and how our societies function, it did not descend equally. As we know, it ravaged some disproportionately: Black communities, Indigenous communities, the incarcerated. And weathering one such disaster does not grant immunity to others, as the family of George Floyd—the American whose killing touched off continent-wide protests about police brutality and racism—learned. Others battered by the twin perils of poverty and Covid or racial disparities and Covid have made the same unhappy discovery. And for hundreds of thousands more, those truths announced in this time have become impossible to ignore. Announced is not the right word: the chasms revealed tell us they have always been there; now they just insist on being seen.

There were five thousand fatal shootings by American police in the past five years. (Canada's problem is a good deal less severe—555 deaths as a result of deadly force between 2000 and 2020—but still adds up to twenty-eight fatalities a year, with Black and Indigenous individuals disproportionately represented.) A number of the killings in both countries were captured on video. It's hard to say why none of those set off a movement, why the great masses were able to see George Floyd's death—and not those others—in a way that galvanized so many into action. Does a rearrangement of the world suddenly allow us to see? Does the space created when we hit pause on productivity suddenly allow us to feel? Does deprivation open our minds to experience some things even as it closes off other experiences we might choose instead?

If disruption is not anything one chooses, deprivation is even less so, least of all in this time and place. Sure, North America in the twenty-first century likes renunciation of the discretionary, recreational variety: lifestyle choices involving voluntary scarcity—the giving up, say, of gluten, sugar, dairy, or caffeine. But outside the domain of physical self-improvement, the idea of constraining ourselves is an unwelcome, and unfamiliar, one. Limitlessness, as Michelle Orange writes, is part of an ethos of our times that has transformed not only the landscape of industry but also the world we all live in—as she puts it, "the values shared by you and me and [Google co-founder] Larry Page."

With a pandemic disrupting schedules, supply chains, rituals of consumer behavior, and the rhythms of our lives, we have had to give up on that idea, at least temporarily. If this leads to shifts in our thinking, it will not have been all bad. Boundless opportunity for some really only seems to come with harsh deprivation for others. Many countries with great numbers of billionaires are also ones with high inequality. The arrival of hard limits to some things has also reminded us—even those with the ability to buy their way out of most problems—that there is happiness to be found without limitlessness.

Benjamin Leszcz's piece, "The Life-Changing Magic of Making Do" seems in some ways written for these times, an admonishment that captures a new reality. "Making do, in times of scarcity, is straightforward," he writes. "If our weekly sugar ration is two hundred grams, then we get by. In the context of abundance, it's complicated. How do we set limits when more, or new, is easily within reach?" That's a question many citizens might ask now, particularly those whose brief flirtation with deprivation has passed. It calls to mind Marshall Sahlins, who in addition to contributing a foundational work on kinship, also wrote about affluence and poverty. "There are two possible courses to affluence," Sahlins posited. "Wants may be 'easily satisfied' either by producing much or desiring little." If the world's landfills offer any clues, modern humans, particularly in the developed world, have tended to lean toward the former. And in the gap between great wants and limited means lies trouble. Whatever the diet books on best-seller lists may say, the answer doesn't lie in fetishizing scarcity, but rather in adjusting our sense of the necessary.

Finding beauty amid constraint is the subject of Christina Sharpe's brief but poignant essay. I read it for the first time in a frigid Toronto church library in February—perhaps my last opportunity to risk chilblains for the pleasure; the church has since been claimed by progress and is to be demolished to make way for new construction. Even on a rereading, especially in this moment of too much precarity, every paragraph startles me awake. Sharpe approaches limitlessness form the other side; she grew up in an American town, Wayne, Pennsylvania, in a Black neighbourhood surrounded by wealthy white neighbourhoods. She writes about notes left by her mother in books that were keyholes offering glimpses of a wider world, an expansive life of the mind. She writes about flowers her mother brought in from the garden. She is talking about race and poverty and beauty and about surviving a world that is unfriendly if not hostile to your existence. (Not every life was free or unpatrolled in the Before Times, we are reminded.) The precision and elegance of her language should open that experience to anyone in any time. But they do so all the more so now, when many are seeking beauty in deprivation—and some, at least, allow themselves the act of imagination to see other peoples' fight to obtain it, against every odd. "What is beauty made of? Attentiveness whenever possible to a kind of aesthetic that escaped violence whenever possible," she writes. It reads a different way in the new world.

Many of these essays do. Some are eerily prescient: Andrew Nikiforuk and Amorina Kingdon's piece on pandemics and progress, published in November 2019, was written when the novel form of a distinctively shaped virus had not yet found its first human host. The pair explored the role of advances in transportation in transmitting the so-called Spanish flu; in the hundred years since, they pointed out, globalization has only shrunk the world further, creating an environment ripe for pandemics. Indeed. "The Unbearable Smugness of Walking," by Michael LaPointe, seemed conceived for a year in which many people, lacking other options for pleasure or exercise or respite from loved ones, reacquainted themselves with the old art of rambling. In it, LaPointe, never one to be taken in by mere charm, applies a keen critical sense to this beloved and unassailable act, parsing the way walking has become romanticized, turned into a self-satisfied pleasure best practised by the comfortable. And again, the essay is difficult to read now without considering that the fate of the walk depends very much on the identity of the walker. A Black man walking without purpose from town to town in many parts of North America today would risk arousing suspicion.

I will not introduce every essay in this book here; they are all wonderful and thought-provoking. But I would like to mention the pieces by Carl Wilson and Andy Lamey. Wilson's piece on the legacy of Michael Jackson gains resonance as efforts continue to think through problematic history. What do we do with difficult figures who have committed crimes or inflicted traumas even while creating important or influential cultural works? The question has acquired urgency as North America grapples with the legacy of a racist past. Wilson argues that Michael Jackson is the Dickens of pop music—colossal in his influence and reach. "Nearly a decade after his death, there are weeks when half the acts on the Billboard chart sound like they're doing MJ imitations," he writes. Is it even possible to write a person like this, or his art, out of history? It's too late to cancel Michael Jackson, he concludes. Wilson was writing in 2019, before the word "cancellation" itself became a lexical grenade, but rephrasing the question doesn't make it any less vexing a conundrum.

Andy Lamey's essay presents an under-discussed dimension of the familiar question of shuttered debate. Free speech has acquired an ugly veneer in recent years, as an issue championed by those driven less by a sense of justice than a desire to ensure space for troublesome ideologies. When 150 prominent figures signed an open letter published in *Harper's* magazine this past summer, the outcry was swift. Open debate, activists for racial or gender justice rightly pointed out, through most of history did not secure for all groups the right to express themselves freely. Why fight for it? The idea that free speech is a distraction at best, and at worst nefarious cover to allow the continuation of injustices, has been taken up by many mainstream voices. But that stance is complicated by the subject of Lamey's essay: the harsh realities for pro-Palestine activists and scholars on campus. In campus after campus, these individuals have seen their events barred; many have lost academic jobs because of the political views they hold. Lamey has long evinced an interest in those who don't belong—his prescient 2011 book *Frontier Justice* illuminated the philosophical and political questions underpinning the global refugee crisis. The people he writes about in this essay are intellectual, rather than political, exiles. Lamey illuminates the plight of these scholars, who are lost in the politics between a social justice–focused left uninterested in fights about free speech, and a free speech–espousing right hostile to the Palestinian cause.

At the heart of some of these questions is how we define those who are like us and those who are different from us, and how we then navigate difference. Those roads, too, lead back to kinship, and to how we circumscribe our communities, whom we call our fellow travellers—the siblings in our canoe. It is not by accident that we have had a collision of flashpoints and failures of late: in public health, the economy, policing, and justice. These are in a sense failures of kinship as well as of good policy, planning, imagination, law. But this difficult moment is also a chance for more constructive conversations. Those conversations need wonks and researchers and lawmakers and citizen groups. They also need writers, essaying in the French sense of the word to think it through. They need at least some voices speaking, or trying to speak, to everybody. There are a lot of us in this sea, which seems suddenly rather more perilous than it did before. Cruise ships, while big enough to hold us, seem the wrong metaphor for the moment. But perhaps we can think of ourselves in so many canoes, helped along by siblings.

HOW FREE IS TOO FREE?: SURVEILLANCE CAPITALISM, MARKET DEMOCRACY, AND THE DANGERS OF MODERN FREEDOM

Michelle Orange

After a fallow period of about fifteen years, in 2014 I returned to driving. Having let my license expire out of pure indolence, I embarked on a process that ended with a road test in deepest Brooklyn. I had no car and no plans to buy one, but within a couple years I was doing more driving than anyone I knew. A needy dog five pounds too big to fly and a sick parent five hundred miles away sent me again and again to the closest rental depot, where I would be handed keys to compact cars of limited but occasionally stark variation. For the same price, I might settle into a vehicle loaded with sixty-seven computers and a heated steering wheel, or a shitbox with no USB port and a tire set to blow on a major Ontario highway. I would search the rental agent's face as she clacked in the relevant data, looking for signs of my fate.

I developed a fondness for the lesser Fords—Fiesta, Focus, Fusion. Solid little numbers with a smooth ride and decent mileage. Much had changed since I last sat behind a wheel: today's cars flash with digital screens and inscrutable features; Google Maps lights the way. Together with the friction went the pleasure of striking down an open road—of feeling free and selfish, gobbling time and space and finite resources. If the fantasy of personal liberty cars once represented was just that, today even the illusion is gone: to drive is simply to travel at greater speed within one's digital carapace, fielding and obeying its endless stream of signals and commands.

Besides, the roads were never, ever open. I learned to game the logistics, to leave one major city before dawn, arrive in the other before the evening crush. Still, every artery and capillary teemed. Gridlock unnerved me less than the relentless flow. *Who* are *all these people? Where are they going?* Having gained some fresh vantage on a clotted freeway, more than once I heard myself muttering that it was all too much. This must be it, I thought: the look and feel of too much freedom.

In an 1819 essay, the Swiss-born writer and politician Benjamin Constant proposed that the ancient ideal of democracy had no place in the modern world, and a new line between personal and political freedom must be drawn. In Sparta and Athens, he wrote, the individual exercised power as a member of the collective, but the collective in turn constrained her every move: "All private actions were submitted to a severe surveillance. No importance was given to individual independence, neither in relation to opinions, nor labor, nor, above all, to religion." Democracy is good, but "individual liberty . . . is the true modern liberty," with political liberty as its guarantee. Modern individuals need authorities "only to give us the general means of instruction which they can supply, as travelers accept from them the main road without being told by them which route to take."

At any rate, true democracy does not scale well. Higher population equals less political influence per capita; to find fulfillment, her place in a bulging order, the modern person must define herself as an individual first, a citizen thereafter. Writing at the close of the Napoleonic wars, Constant celebrated commerce as an instrument of both personal and political power: war precedes commerce and commerce replaces war, giving those weary of conflict's burdens a better option, "a milder and surer means of engaging the interest of others to agree to what suits his own."

Constant also recognizes the danger of modern freedom, the notion that "absorbed in the enjoyments and pursuits of our private independence and in pursuit of our particular interests, we should surrender our right to share in political power too easily. The holders of authority are only too anxious to encourage us to do so." Constant's authority-holders are implicitly political: the party leaders, legislators, and government bodies reorganizing many Western societies. No monarchs or despots but no democratic institutions either should be believed in their claim to provide citizens every happiness, "to spare us all sort of troubles, except those of obeying and paying!"

Constant came to be considered a classicist in his own right, emblematic of what is known as classical liberalism, the current affiliation of choice for the likes of Paul Ryan and Jordan Peterson. Having been checked, in the wake of two world wars and an economic collapse, by the liberal principles now associated with the far left, the ideas of Constant and his fellow classical liberals John Stuart Mill and Adam Smith were resurrected in the late twentieth century as "neoliberalism," a label, as critic Stephen Metcalf has observed, that has been considered a catchall political slur, "a term without any analytic power." In fact, writes Metcalf, neoliberalism names and organizes the dominant ideology of our time, in which the veneration of free markets and morbid individualism has eroded societies and "invaded the grit of our personal lives." Metcalf believes it could not have been otherwise, that "there was, from the beginning, an inevitable relationship between the utopian ideal of the free market and the dystopian present in which we find ourselves; between the market as unique discloser of value and guardian of liberty, and our current descent into post-truth and illiberalism."

The question of how free is too free may have boggled democracies throughout history, but never in quite the way it now boggles ours. The current predicament stands within the life of every individual, pointing at irreconcilable angles her own interests, those of the public she constitutes, and of the planet she inhabits. It might leave her muttering, on a coursing interstate, about autonomy run amok; or ranting about damn liberals at a Steve Bannon rally, as one Cincinnati woman did this spring. "If you want to take it back, it's citizen involvement—you can take the trash out," Bannon told the woman. "Never in my life did I think I'd like to see a dictator," the woman replied. "But if there's going to be one, I want it to be Trump!"

Bannon clapped. The crowd roared.

In her livid, methodical account of the rise of what she calls "surveillance capitalism," Harvard Business School professor Shoshana Zuboff blames neoliberalism, among other things, for the rise of Google and its offspring. She describes a study of 1,400 law review articles: published between 1980 and 2005, their unifying proposition was that of government as coercive body, and industry regulation as a form of authoritarian rule. They pointed to self-regulation as a solution to the threat posed by meddling governments: firms could set their own terms, evaluate their own compliance with those terms, "and even judge their own conduct," writes Zuboff. "By the time of Google's public offering in 2004, self-regulation was fully enshrined within government and across the business community as the most effective tool for regulation without coercion and the antidote to any inclination toward collectivism and the centralization of power."

According to *The Age of Surveillance Capitalism*, this was a key step in our becoming far less free than we believe ourselves to be. In order to finally turn a profit, in the wake of the dot-com crash, Google made a pioneering discovery: the people using its free search engine were generating a surplus of data; rendered as a commodity, human experience could be subjected to market dynamics and sold as what Zuboff calls "behavioral futures." One hears this now widely known practice described as a matter of *mining, scraping, extraction*—an act of physical force. In fact, surveillance capitalism relies on its invisibility, a touch that, when it is perceived at all, might be mistaken for a caress. Under the banner of increased convenience, connectivity, freedom, and personalization, companies like Google, Facebook, and Amazon turn individuals into lucrative but expendable data sets, useful in so far as predictions about their future behaviour yield a market value.

Just as they depended on the erosion of democratic processes for their success, these companies operate to anti-democratic effect. Together they form what Zuboff, an ardent neologist, calls "Big Other," an entity manifest in the apparently friendly, benign TV that watches you, the wristband that monitors you, the house that knows you, the being that answers your questions about the weather and farts on command. Big Other "acts on behalf of an unprecedented assembly of commercial operations that must modify human behavior as a condition of commercial success. It replaces legitimate contract, the rule of law, politics, and social trust with a new form of sovereignty and its privately administered regime of reinforcements."

Weighted by repetition and Zuboff's thudding way with metaphor, in its sum *The Age of Surveillance Capitalism* is a fearful document: focused, meticulous, and deeply persuasive. Written in a style at once breathless and didactic, it reads like a digital paranoiac's dream: they really are out to get you. They pretty much already have you, Zuboff makes plain, and the bargain we have unwittingly made to be counted not as citizens or individuals but users and clickers—broodmares on the data farm—has furthered social and cultural divides, our alienation from ourselves and one other. Not governments but corporations and finance conglomerates now hold ultimate authority, and they are focused in their efforts to "drive and preserve an extreme free-market agenda at the expense of democracy."

Speaking with Naomi Klein this spring, Zuboff returned to a central theme of her book: to beat surveillance capitalism, we must "activate the resources of our democratic institutions." I may have imagined Klein wincing when Zuboff said we still needed capitalism, that in fact there is "an imperfect equilibrium that we call 'market democracy' that can serve society well." Surveillance capitalism, she takes care to show, did not emerge in a vacuum: Larry Page's vision of a world in which our whole lives would be searchable "perfectly reflects the history of capitalism," an enterprise based in "taking things that live outside the market sphere and declaring their new life as market commodities." But Zuboff does not see a company like Google as a natural extension of the capitalist project and its quest for perpetual growth. Rather, the surveillance merchants are a rogue, totalizing mutation of the real thing. They have overturned the traditional capitalist order, pushing us "toward a society in which capitalism does not function as a means to economic or political institutions."

The example of this traditional ideal to which Zuboff most often returns is that of Henry Ford, and his belief that "mass production begins in the perception of a public need." As Zuboff tells it, people wanted affordable cars, Ford made them, and therein lay a happy reciprocity. Democracy not only survived but lived to modulate this new market form. By insisting on the novelty of surveillance capitalism, "a boundary-less form that ignores older distinctions between market and society, market and world, or market and person," Zuboff refuses the notion that all of those older distinctions were built to break down in precisely the way they did. She fails to reckon with the extent to which the capitalist norms she endorses shifted not just the economy but the culture (not to mention the health of the planet), creating the climate of self-interest, consumption, and limitlessness that helped shape the world and the values shared by you and me and Larry Page.

As of 2018, there were 1.26 vehicles on the road for every licensed driver in the US, a threshold some call "peak motorization." The American auto industry has already died and resurrected itself once—as a loan financier. Following the 2017 announcement that Ford would cease production of almost all its passenger cars, CEO Jim Hackett declared that the company's future lay in surveillance. Their one hundred million customers had been generating untapped data all this time, said Hackett, their choices and habits unmonetized, every turn, stop, and speeding jag lost to the market winds. And where's the sense in that?

What is market democracy? What is *democracy*? The answer to the first question is often posed in deceptively simple, amiable terms, as in Zuboff's précis of Thomas Piketty: not to be eaten raw, "capitalism, like sausage, is meant to be cooked by a democratic society." In the spring of 2019, Elizabeth Warren told Stephen Colbert that she believes in markets, "but markets need rules and they need a cop on the beat to enforce those rules." Such distillations seem unlikely to inspire an audience increasingly divided into those that see market democracy as either a contradiction or a redundancy in terms.

In her third feature documentary, filmmaker and activist Astra Taylor poses to various scholars (including Cornel West, Silvia Federici, and Wendy Brown), civilians, schoolchildren, and at least one refugee, some version of her third documentary feature's title question: *What Is Democracy?* The result is a sort of Socratic journey, one that moves between Greece, the US, and points in between, finding everywhere more questions and a growing gap between the democratic ideal and reality. As challenging as it is accessible, the film is loose, digressive, organized not by story but by a series of ideas and observations: about what democracy has been and what it should be; where it has gone wrong and why it is destined to fail; about how to make democracy out of an undemocratic people and whether it is worth the faithful pursuit it demands.

The main framing device is Taylor's conversation with Federici in Siena, where the pair contemplate an Ambrogio Lorenzetti fresco titled "The Allegory and Effects of Good and Bad Government." Federici describes the tri-panelled painting, which was commissioned by local government in the 1330s, as propaganda for Siena's oligarchy, the ruling class in one of the earliest merchant-banking societies. Asserting their values as the holiest and their leadership as a guarantee of peace and prosperity was a matter of maintaining power. In Siena, the seeds of capitalism took deeper root than those of democracy.

If, as Federici claims, democracy must be defined from below, how far down—and across—is it prudent or even plausible to go? It wasn't majority rule, after all, that in the United States ended slavery or integrated schools, as West reminds us, and until the last century, even the most forward-looking democracy disenfranchised half of its population. A growing quantity of evidence suggests fewer and fewer Americans understand or care to defend democratic values and norms, a development that feels folded into the partisan crevasse threatening to swallow even the memory of civilized discourse. Over the last decade, conservative legislators in states including Texas, Georgia, and Michigan have acted to purge the words "democracy" and "democratic" from K-12 social studies curricula descriptions of American government.

One can imagine Taylor's film having a place in the classroom, though one would first have to imagine the kind of a classroom this country appears bent on destroying. As political theorist Wendy Brown points out, to define democracy from below we must first cultivate a taste for it across the vast middle, create cultural amenability toward a system it is not in our nature to sustain. It's not a task for Russian bots or the new robber barons, who would love to spare us every trouble except that of obeying and paying. It is not a matter of engagement as we know it now—a like, a comment, a thing to buy off Instagram. The means are phenomenal, obscure by design but rooted, perhaps, in the perception of almighty public need. The bargain, as Taylor makes plain, has never been clean. If not worth making, it demands a democratic sort of pondering: the willingness of a majority of individuals to educate themselves, act accordingly, and be free.

IT'S TOO LATE TO
CANCEL MICHAEL JACKSON

Carl Wilson

It was an ugly rumour that circulated for years, but fans of
the great artist were in denial until evidence emerged that
seemed impossible to refute. I'm talking about the research
that came out last week showing that when Charles Dickens
was dumping his wife of a quarter century, the mother of
his ten children, in order to pursue his affair with an eigh-
teen-year-old actress, he tried to have his spouse shut away
in a mental asylum. It wasn't an uncommon cruelty for men
in Victorian England to commit against perfectly sound-
minded partners. Dickens only failed in his efforts because
the humanitarian-minded doctor friend he approached
turned him down. Disgusting as the tale is, it's hard to believe
it will do more than glancing damage to Dickens' standing.
Scholars took decades to come around to the truth about his
long-running dalliance with the actress, but once they did,
few communities chose to shut down their annual produc-
tions of *A Christmas Carol*. Dickens remains too central to
literary culture, while the people he hurt (he was also a crap
father) are way back in the nineteenth-century London fog.
None of which makes what nearly befell Catherine Dickens
less awful.

For all the emotions and issues that will come up as HBO broadcasts the harrowing *Leaving Neverland* documentary about Michael Jackson's alleged child sexual abuse this weekend, it's a stubborn, inconvenient fact that Jackson was to modern popular music and dance what Dickens was to the Victorian novel—a parallel you'll find strange only if you don't care for modern pop music. *Thriller* continues today to be the best-selling album of all time around the world, and estimates of between sixty-six million and one hundred million copies sold don't account for the unimaginable numbers of cassette-taped and file-traded versions in people's collections, from Boston to Botswana. Nearly a decade after his death, there are weeks when half the acts on the Billboard chart sound like they're doing MJ imitations. In terms of global reach, recognition, and influence, no one but the Beatles and Elvis can compare. And John Lennon physically assaulted his first wife, and almost beat a man to death for suggesting he was gay. Elvis started dating his wife-to-be when Priscilla Ann Wagner was fourteen and he was twenty-four.

I'm not raising these cases to excuse Jackson of the horrifying allegations that are made against him in the documentary, not to mention the charges he evaded in court during his life. The stories of the two alleged abuse survivors in the film are extremely detailed and convincing. They're especially disturbing if, like me and many others, you once performed Olympian mental gymnastics to sustain some faith in Jackson's relative innocence.

Still, I put Jackson alongside the likes of Lennon and Dickens to point out that some cases test the limits of righteous dismissal. It can feel like swift and satisfying justice when people on social media reacting to reports of bigotry or abuse, for instance, declare the accused "cancelled"—persona non grata, never to be spoken of again except to mete out further censure. But to embezzle a phrase from the 2008 financial crisis, are some figures too big to cancel? Too consequential to write out of the record, especially when they're deceased, and beyond any effective sanction? When I mentioned to a friend that I was writing this piece, she remarked, "I'll cope with Michael Jackson when I'm finished processing Charlie Chaplin." Which, her tone implied, might be never.

Alternatively, you may call to mind Miles Davis. Or James Brown. (Bill Cosby, though still living, might also stalk your thoughts, but while his was a watershed career, I suspect his comedy relied too heavily on personal likability for it to rebound from all the repellant revelations.) Not to mention the groundbreaking white feminist writers who were nonetheless racists, such as the eugenicist Charlotte Perkins Gilman, or Virginia Woolf, whose record is marred by early anti-Semitism.

It's one thing to blacklist the music of someone like R Kelly. He's alive, and so far unpunished for his alleged multitudes of crimes. It's necessary to undo the complicity that so much of the music industry and the media indulged him with for so long. But additionally, while his music loomed large in 1990s and 2000s R&B, it's in the end not indispensable. I don't mean that Jackson or the Beatles get a magic "genius" pass— that title, so freighted with Great Man archetypes, obscures more than it illuminates. At best, it should be used to describe the momentary visitations of the sublime that arise in a particular creative act, not as a label affixed permanently to a person, removing them to an untouchable sphere. Still, there are points where the apparently irresistible force of moral outrage runs into immovable objects of cultural history.

There are plenty of Jackson songs that will feel radioactive from now on. All the ones with children's choirs. Certainly "The Lost Children" and "Do You Know Where Your Children Are," which now sound like Jackson accusing society at large of the very sins he was committing, as if he couldn't get them off his mind. As my colleague Jack Hamilton points out, Jackson's fixation on children was all over his work. But not so much on the stuff that really counted. And all the grandiose paranoia and defensiveness that riddled his songs in the 1990s might sound excruciating now, if the persecution Jackson was railing against was simply justice. But a lot of it sounded painful in the first place. While fans can make persuasive arguments for some of those later songs and albums, such as *Dangerous* and *HIStory*, that's not the Michael Jackson who changed the musical world, the Jackson of "I Want You Back" and "Rock With You" and "Billie Jean." I'd similarly be happy never again to hear the Beatles' "Run for Your Life," in which Lennon threatens to kill a woman if she cheats on him. Like-wise, knowing what we do about Chuck Berry's sexual trans-gressions, we can do fine without "Sweet Little Sixteen" and, for all our sakes, "My Ding-a-Ling." But pretending to throw that foundational performer and songwriter's work as a whole into the landfill would be an empty rhetorical flourish—if Ameri-can music matters to you, it's not a genuine option.

Obviously, individuals can and should make their own calls. When Hannah Gadsby declared in her *Nanette* Netf-lix special that she was done with Picasso and his misogyny forever, I had no objection, save that I felt like the culture in general had kind of decided that about Picasso a while ago (though I confess I'm keeping the *Guernica*). I also sympa-thize when anyone exasperated by the parade of offensive straight male notables decides to concentrate their attention instead on the huge numbers of brilliant non-male, non-straight artists who've been denied the spotlight. That's a needed correction no matter what. (The finest essay wrestling intimately with these issues is Claire Dederer's 2017 "What Do We Do With the Art of Monstrous Men?" She's expanding it into what should be a crucial book.)

There are immediate practical questions. Music often invades our ears in public, uninvited. In the near future, Jack-son's songs shouldn't be played on the radio or in any other way that might cause people who've been abused to encounter his music against their will. Their potential trauma outweighs any other consideration, at least for a while. Hell, I don't want to hear that music anytime soon myself, though I bet I will.

Ultimately, though, Michael Jackson won't disappear. Which means we'll continue to reckon with how to think about him, and our own moral instincts. How do we hold in our minds simultaneously that Jackson allegedly did reprehensible things to small children and that he also brought widespread joy and changed the sound of global pop? Neither fact alters the other. Any desire I once might have had to minimize the alleged crimes has been wrung out of me. But as it distorts reality to designate people geniuses—as if that legitimizes everything about them—we should hesitate to call people monsters. That's succumbing to the opposite fantasy: that a person who's done despicable things is purely a vehicle for those acts, consumed by malevolence, and corrupt and inauthentic in all other respects. This dehumanization protects us from fearing that we have anything in common with them, or bothering to understand them any further.

The London-based criminologist and psychologist Julia Shaw published a book this month called *Evil: The Science Behind Humanity's Dark Side*, in which she advocates that we collectively stop using the word evil itself. It halts the conversation, she proposes, exactly where it should begin. She's not making a case for moral relativism. Rather, she argues that dark urges are far more universal than we admit, while extreme manifestations are rarer than our media-fevered brains imagine. Most murders, for example, are the one-time results of conflicts that spin out of control, not the handiwork of devoted killers, and most murderers immediately regret it. In her chapter specifically about pedophilia, she discusses how the taboos around facing or addressing the disorder—one survey discovered that some impulses in that direction can be found in up to 6 percent of men and 2 percent of women—make it almost impossible for those who have it to seek treatment, lest they be arrested for the mere admission.

This paradox makes it more likely that actual children will be abused. And still, most who feel those attractions never do act on them, because they remain human beings who realize it's wrong. Not monsters.

I cannot speculate on how Michael Jackson might have struggled with the man in the mirror, though one wonders whether any of his managers, friends, or family ever hazarded speaking with him honestly about his alleged problems instead of automatically bolstering his denials. Frankly, I'm nervous even passing along Shaw's research, lest you make the wrong inferences about me—which is another of the syndromes around "evil" that she identifies, that anyone daring to bring up such toxic subjects risks being stigmatized themselves. But I think that there are corresponding self-defeating patterns in how we confront these figures in our culture. It's vital that someone like R Kelly, again, is being charged and will hopefully be prosecuted for the years of abuse he's allegedly perpetrated against young women. But it doesn't fix what allowed Kelly to carry on for so long. The cultural compulsion to set artists and celebrities up as gods and heroes, and then desperately defend those illusions, isn't cured when one or many are finally ejected from the pantheon. I can't watch *Leaving Neverland* and not think about that.

Listening to the families' stories, I noticed how, as soon as they came into Jackson's orbit, everything became kind of dreamlike and unreal. It's easy to condemn the parents who failed to protect their children from the star, and even facilitated the relationships. But it seems normal to me. Have you had a period when you suddenly fell in with the cool crowd, or even one person who was glamorous to you? Such magnetism can blind and derange. Perhaps when you look back you also feel guilty about what you did under that sway, whether it was being neglectful of other friends and family or taking part in something dumb and self-destructive because the pretty people were doing it, telling yourself it was fine.

These boundaries are far more unstable for children. What unsettles me in hearing *Leaving Neverland*'s two alleged survivors, now grown men, is that despite everything twisted about it, they're each telling a love story. It's why it took them so long to admit the truth to themselves—not until after Jackson's death—and why they even testified falsely in his defense. Referring to the 2005 trial, Wade Robson's wife says in the film, "Love is so powerful."

These families' stories reflect the whole culture's relationship with stars, and their relationships with us—stories of idolization and exploitation, of projection and possession, of opportunism and rationalization. And of the wreckage left behind. When you love a star, inherently you're loving a person who doesn't exist, a figment of image creation and your own manipulated yearnings. In Jackson's case, that goes double. He seemed so dissociated in the ways he presented himself through the last half of his life that it's hard to guess how much of reality he was experiencing. Was he a person who didn't exist even for himself?

If there's anything *Leaving Neverland* makes me want to get rid of entirely, it is child stardom, which mangled this man's psyche and went on to be a lure for the children and families who attached themselves to him. I could wish the same about stardom in general, but that would be another rhetorical flourish. Stardom, that atrocity waiting to happen, is what the machinery of this culture is geared to produce, more so than any particular artwork or entertainment. It is beyond the control of any of us, performer or fan, sinner or saint. Though if there are any, I'd guess the saints have better things to do.

THE UNBEARABLE SMUGNESS OF WALKING

Michael LaPointe

Lifespan, a maker of fitness equipment, claims that a treadmill desk will boost my creativity. The company's website, where I can purchase its basic model for $1,099, features an inspirational quote from Nietzsche: "All truly great thoughts are conceived while walking." Researchers agree on the connection between an acute mind and legs in motion. Studies have shown that we do better on tests of memory and attention during or after exercise. Studies have also shown that a walker's mental meandering is unusually conducive to innovation. "Above all, do not lose your desire to walk," Søren Kierkegaard advised, and I'm hardly the only writer who has heeded the call, putting one foot before the other in search of fresh insights and breakthroughs in knotty arguments.

Before the advent of scientific evidence and philosophical guidance on the subject, literary odes to the creative and health benefits of walking flourished. No one has been more tireless in reviving the history of exhortations to join the "Order of Walkers" than the British editor and BBC producer Duncan Minshull. Back in 2000, he co-edited *The Vintage Book of Walking: A Glorious, Funny and Indispensable Collection*, which could also boast of being the most comprehensive anthology of such proselytizing, spanning fiction and nonfiction. It was reissued in 2014 as *While Wandering: A Walking Companion*.

Minshull has now followed up with the considerably trimmer *Beneath My Feet: Writers on Walking*, which gathers thirty-six testimonies to walking's invigorating literary power in particular. Writers from Petrarch to Franz Kafka to Will Self have recorded their enthusiasm for, in Minshull's words, "ambling, rambling, tramping, trekking, stomping and striding." Higher-quality endorsements of the creative value of walking than these would be hard to find. Yet the more I read, the more questions this twenty-first-century renaissance of pedestrian evangelism raised in my mind. No, I haven't lost my desire, Kierkegaard, but I think about my desire differently—and wish I didn't.

Beneath My Feet, though it reaches back to the fourteenth century, hits its stride in the Romantic period. That's when walking and writing became inextricably entwined. In a 1902 essay, the critic and biographer (and Virginia Woolf's father) Leslie Stephen argues that Romanticism, with its sublime visions of the natural world, "was obviously due in great part, if not mainly, to the renewed practice of walking." It's easy to picture William Wordsworth—who wrote in his preface to *Lyrical Ballads* that "the essential passions of the heart find a better soil" in a rustic environment—stomping out *The Prelude*, his legs serving as his metronome. In an 1822 essay, William Hazlitt writes of how Samuel Taylor Coleridge could "convert a landscape into a didactic poem or a Pindaric ode." Putting boots on the ground was a way of pledging allegiance to a poetic freedom available only in open space.

Even among writers who soon exchanged the country for the city, the Romantic conception of walking as the essential literary act persisted. The figure of the flâneur, whom Charles Baudelaire defined as a "passionate spectator" of the urban scene, emerged in late-nineteenth-century Paris and produced a literature that turned its back on nature, immersed instead in grime and city steam. Wordsworth aspired to an unshackled imaginative vision, Baudelaire to a voluptuous delirium, but they shared the physical mechanics of literary production: walk, observe, write.

The image of the writer-walker was well enough entrenched by the twentieth century that a walk could be consciously undertaken as a literary apprenticeship. In a 1975 reminiscence about New York, the novelist and essayist Edward Hoagland recalls how he stalked the streets of his hometown, first "to smell the yeasty redolence of the Nabisco factory" and then "to West Twelfth Street to sniff the police stables." The author was inhaling the raw stuff that would fuel creativity: "I knew that every mile I walked, the better writer I'd be."

Literary walking took on a new political energy at the turn of the twenty-first century. "Thinking is generally thought of as doing nothing in a production-orientated culture," Rebecca Solnit writes in an excerpt from her book *Wanderlust: A History of Walking* (2001), "and doing nothing is hard to do . . . the something closest to doing nothing is walking." Viewed from this perspective, a walk isn't just good creative exercise. It's a form of protest against buying and selling, against goal-directed busyness. It's an autonomous march in opposition to the stream of conformity. And like the slow-food movement, slow-transport literature posits walking as an important part of imagining a more sustainable future.

In his new book, *Walking: One Step at a Time*, the Norwegian writer and explorer Erling Kagge follows Solnit in highlighting the political implications of walking. Not that his kind of walk remotely resembles "doing nothing." Kagge is the first person to have completed the Three Poles Challenge (North, South, and Mount Everest) on foot. He's traversed the New York City sewer system, cultivating "inner silence" along his gruelling way and enjoying the familiar litany of inspirational benefits. He celebrates "a healthy stretch of [the] legs, a kick of endorphins," which evoke meditations unavailable to non-walkers, who also "don't notice the wind, the smells, the weather, nor the shifting light" from within their cars. While walking, he feels his thoughts freeing up, "a bubbling between my ears, new solutions to questions that have been plaguing me."

What Kagge wants to stress, though, is that he writes in reaction to the modern menaces of high speed and convenience that threaten inner silence. "Sitting is about the desire of those in power that we should participate in growing the GDP," he writes, "as well as the corporate desire that we should consume as much as possible and rest whenever we aren't doing so." To walk is to strike out against the culture: "It is among the most radical things you can do."

But just how radical is the writer-walker resurgence that Minshull hoped for twenty years ago and has watched come to pass? Like protesting, walking ought to be among the most democratic of activities. Look closely at the genre, though, and you'll find that the writer-walker has a way of claiming a surprisingly exclusive status.

Henry David Thoreau—whom Kagge salutes as "one of the most central proponents of walking" and to whom Minshull grants plenty of space in both of his anthologies—makes a lyrical companion as he strolls beneath the "pure elastic heaven" of a wintry sky. But dipping further into Minshull's excerpt of his essay "A Winter's Walk," I found the "traveller," as Thoreau calls himself, not quite as inclusive as I'd imagined him to be. In the "wild scenes" of nature, Thoreau comes upon a group of poor labourers out in the open air. He pauses to observe how one of the men "does not make the scenery less wild, more than the jays and muskrats, but stands there as a part of it"—more natural backdrop than fellow traveller. Even as Thoreau grants that the man "too is a worshiper of the unseen," he suggests the writer-wanderer is a type apart.

Minshull nods to the fact that this restless, creative adventuring isn't available to all. An excerpt from the writer Lauren Elkin's *Flâneuse* (2016) points out that the feminine form of flâneur doesn't even appear in most French dictionaries. To walk alone in nineteenth-century Paris, George Sand had to disguise herself in men's clothing. The costume gave her a freedom that activated her imagination: "I could create a whole novel going from one end of town to another." Very briefly, Virginia Woolf looks as though she will be the heroic exception, as we see her stepping out alone into "the champagne brightness of the air" to relish "darkness and lamplight." And yet, she tells us, this daring nocturnal stroll takes place between 4 and 6 pm.

The Pakistani-British novelist Kamila Shamsie's words remain true: "A woman walking alone after midnight is always too conscious of being alone to properly inhabit that space which is solitude." In a similar vein, the writer Garnette Cadogan's "Walking While Black"—which you won't find in Minshull's recent anthology—describes the "cop-proof wardrobe" that enables safe public walking: "Light-colored oxford shirt. V-neck sweater. Khaki pants. Chukkas. Sweatshirt or T-shirt with my university insignia." His essay asks us to consider how a literary creation can germinate on a stroll when "the sidewalk [is] a minefield."

As I sampled the genre, as well as countless articles and ads attesting to the creative effects of walking, I began to feel uneasy about the proselytizing mission. Is membership in the "Order of Walkers" quite the liberation it seems? Even those lucky enough to belong to its ranks might ask themselves how undistracted solitude and untethered mind-wandering can prosper when walking is constantly justified in terms of productivity. The twenty-first-century walking revival may have begun as a political critique, but it has found itself co-opted by the very forces it seeks to resist.

The more conscious writers become of its creative benefits, the more walking takes on the quality of goal-driven labour, the very thing we are meant to be marching against. The hazard was always there. William Hazlitt gestures toward it in his entry in *Beneath My Feet*. "When I am in the country," he writes, "I wish to vegetate like the country." If he begins to feel that he has to produce a piece of writing from his walks, like "my old friend Coleridge," then he's "making a toil of a pleasure."

Solnit champions something like Hazlitt's vegetating when she writes that walking "produces nothing but thoughts, experiences, arrivals." And yet again and again in the literature of walking, a stroll is portrayed as a working method. Minshull tempts us with the possibility that, while walking, "thoughts are stirred, which leads to creativity, to a verse or a paragraph," so how can a writer ever walk for walking's sake? Even Hazlitt, who suggests what it might mean to vegetate, made an excellent piece of writing from the idea. Solnit, too, put her thoughts, experiences, and arrivals to use in her book.

Much of this essay was conceived while I was walking. Sometimes I would deliberately set out to inhabit solitude, hoping my ideas would cohere. At other times, I found myself mulling over paragraphs like this one as I went about my day—strolling to the coffee shop or grocery store. Somewhere along the way, I realized that, as a writer, I never walk without working. On Wordsworth's better soil, I've built an office. In Kagge's inner silence, my keyboard chatters away. I don't need to buy anything from LifeSpan, because I already walk upon an invisible treadmill desk, constantly channeling the powers beneath my feet into the next paycheque. What would it mean, for once, simply to walk and say nothing about it?

THE LONELINESS OF INFERTILITY

Alexandra Kimball

The summer after our third miscarriage, Jeremy convinced me to go to a fancy party for his work. He thought that dressing up and eating a nice meal in a ballroom with other dressed-up people might distract me. I sat in my cocktail dress—too tight on my post-IVF bloat—and held my husband's hand under the table. Occasionally, a waiter would pass by with canapés and I'd grab one with my free hand. The table was buzzing with wine-leavened conversation, with introductions and interruptions and compliments, especially for the women, who wore a lot of modest necklines and black and navy—the assured unchicness of those who do not need to impress. They generated an air of capability and confidence, of success.

I desperately, desperately did not want to talk to any of them. Over the previous four years, socializing had become my biggest problem, second only to infertility. If you had asked me about my social life, I would have said, "It does not exist," though, in fact, all I did was talk to other people—in support groups on Facebook and the forum sections of infertility websites. I'd wake up in the morning and log on and read and write all day with hundreds of infertile women. We'd share details of our miscarriages, our IVF results, our searches for surrogates, and reply to one another's queries and stories in turn. But as soon as I logged off, I'd forget all about these women. Which is not to say I found these groups useless: though I wasn't happy about my condition, I was certainly grateful to have a place I could discuss it. But the circumstances of these conversations made them seem ghostly and unreal, in a way that talking with other women, even about other shitty and gendered topics, never had.

Still, the outside world—I thought of anything non-infertility-related as "outside" and still do—was way worse. Somewhere along the four-year way, my outside friends had retreated. I'd see them every once in a while, but they felt remote, far off in their own galaxies of pregnancy, baby raising, or simply not being infertile. I backed off too. Not infrequently, I'd think of one of these women and feel a sudden hurt, but I preferred this pain to the sharp vertigo I experienced whenever they said something to remind me of the new difference in me, my distance. Social life presented an agonizing conundrum: my infertility was the only thing in my life, and no one, apart from other infertile women, ever wanted to talk about it.

At Jeremy's work party, I was trying to silently project a sense of my private agony, but eventually, the woman seated beside me tapped me on the hand and asked me my name. "Do you have any kids?"

"No," I said.

"Do you plan on having them?" she asked. Her expression was quizzical, slightly amused.

"We can't," I said. "We've had three miscarriages."

Despite being clinical, correct, the word miscarriage, like the word infertility, suggests the particular unruliness of the female body. And even given our culture's nominal feminism (I would have been shocked if any woman at that party rejected being labelled a feminist), there is a perpetual undercurrent of disgust about female genitals and organs. "I tend to regard the female organ as something unclean or as a wound," wrote French surrealist Michel Leiris, "but dangerous in itself, like everything bloody, mucous, infected."

Saying miscarriage out loud was like putting my uterus on the table, bleeding and scarred and radiating misuse. Tears and death and not a small amount of sex. I felt vulgar dropping this bit of feminine gore into the lighthearted civility of the room.

I understood the irony: I had no more exposed my uterus by talking about my lack of children than any other woman who mentions "having kids" does. All children, living or dead, come from bloody uteruses and vaginas—things polite people don't discuss—but the logic of misogyny, which carves out a space of relative respect for some mothers (especially the wealthy, white, and married), means we usually agree to forget this. The beauty of the child erases its origins in the female body and sexuality. But when these parts go wrong and there is no child, nothing is redeemed. It's just the spectre of the female body and sexuality: blood, mucous, infection. Death.

A few moments passed. The woman's mouth opened and closed over the empty air. The waiter came by again, and I plucked a canapé from a round tray. Open, closed, open, closed, like she was gulping air. "Oh," she finally said before rushing off to the washroom or something. I didn't see her again. I still don't know who she was or why she responded the way she did. Her chair remained empty all night, and whenever I looked at it, I wanted to laugh. It was funny, really: a literal instantiation of my isolation.

From her first recorded mentions, the infertile female was a monster. The Babylonian Atrahasis epic, from the eighteenth century BCE, describes a conflict between the gods and the overpopulated world of men, during which the gods flooded the Earth. Eventually repenting for this destruction, the deities restored humankind to the Earth, with a built-in safeguard against overpopulation: "Let there be a third group of people. [Let there be] fertile women and barren women. Let there be the Pagittu-demon among the people and let her snatch the child from the lap of the mother." The demon, writes the University of Pennsylvania Museum's Erle Lichty, was the lion-headed demoness Lamashtu, barren and envious, who caused infertility, miscarriage, and infant death.

The Hebrew Testament of Solomon describes the demon Obizuth—her name in Middle Eastern mythology, Abyzou, is derived from the word for abyss—as a fusion of woman and beast: "her glance was altogether bright and greeny, and her hair was tossed wildly like a dragon's; and the whole of her limbs were invisible." Abyzou was barren, and she confessed that her envy of women who could bear children motivated her murderous hauntings: "[B]y night I sleep not, but go my rounds all over the world, and visit women in childbirth.... [I]f I am lucky, I strangle the child."

The art of this period depicts these demons as serpentine, the unruly, unnatural appearance of such female forms symbolizing their rebuke to traditional femininity.

Beginning in the Renaissance, many Europeans became absorbed in representations of witches, who were frequently accused of kidnapping children and causing miscarriages and stillbirths. The witch hunts in Europe and North America were a touchstone for late-twentieth-century feminist historians, who rightfully noted how the accused often defied the conventional female gender roles of the era: many exhibited the unwomanly characteristics of anger or promiscuity, for instance. But few have emphasized how prominently female barrenness figured in the witch trials, how infertile and childless women were considered both particularly vulnerable to infestation by Satanic spirits and prone to acts of witchcraft themselves.

A seeming bright spot: the Old Testament had, on its surface, a good deal of sympathy for infertile women. (The invocation "Sing, O barren woman!" compares the plight of the chosen people of Israel to the sorrow of an infertile wife.) But in these tales women are described as passive instruments of their reproductive fate: "self-controlled, pure, working at home, kind, and submissive to their own husbands." Thus emerged the only acceptable image of the infertile woman: the pining religious supplicant, barren but virtuous.

As with the literary and religious portrayal of women as a whole, the infertile feminine was split into two opposing archetypes: Abyzou, and the pious Hannah, who after many years of infertility and prayer would go on to mother the prophet Samuel. Angry and vengeful versus passive, silent, and hopeful—public images of female infertility are one or the other to this day.

Feminism—and, in particular, the movement for reproductive rights—has long been either dismissive of or outright hostile to the plight of infertile women. The roots of the reproductive rights movement are not actually in choice—at least, not in the universal, expansive way in which modern feminists talk about choice. Rather, some early advocates of birth control and abortion in the West were concerned with limiting maternity, especially for poor, disabled, and racialized populations (particularly Black and Indigenous women).

In the early and middle twentieth century, feminists fought for and celebrated new technologies in birth control—first, barrier methods like cervical caps and condoms, and then the first generation of contraceptive pills. However, this early feminist project was inextricable from the larger cultural anxiety about the precariousness of race and class in an era marked by mass immigration, incipient civil rights for Black Americans, and the rise of unions.

Margaret Sanger—best known for starting the American Birth Control League, the precursor to Planned Parenthood—founded birth-control clinics and published pamphlets on sexual education during an era when even the idea that women might want to have sex for reasons other than reproduction was blasphemous. But her ultimate enthusiasm for contraception was inseparable from a larger conversation about how modern nations might better society through population control. "If we are to develop in America a new race with a racial soul," she wrote in 1920, "we must not encourage reproduction beyond our capacity to assimilate our numbers so as to make the coming generation into such physically fit, mentally capable, socially alert individuals as are the ideal of a democracy."

Sanger's statements would later be regarded as foundational in laws, often motivated by eugenics, enacted in the US in thirty-three states, that forcibly sterilized at least 65,000 citizens, a large proportion of whom were Black, from the 1900s to until as recently as the 1970s. In Canada, similar laws saw the compulsory sterilization of thousands of women—the majority Indigenous—up until the 1970s; Indigenous women report that coerced sterilizations continue to this day.

Mainstream attention—not just among feminists but across our culture—continues to focus on upper-class white women's infertility even now, usually in the context of scientific advances in fertility medicine. This makes it easier than ever for the public to view infertility not as a general women's health issue but as a type of malaise of the privileged. It also plays directly into racist and classist beliefs that poor women and non-white women are "hyperfertile"—unthinking reproducers who are closer to fertile nature than white women and should be encouraged to have fewer, rather than more, children. (Black women actually experience higher rates of infertility than white women.)

But as a matter of policy it is primarily white middle- to upper-class women who can access health-care services to address their infertility. Across North America, free or low-cost women's health clinics—themselves all too few and far between—will provide birth control, early-pregnancy care, and abortion-referral services but rarely treatment for infertility. (In Canada, only Ontario and Quebec cover some IVF treatments, for instance.)

This exclusion from our public narratives about and public policies for infertility is self-reinforcing: because most academic studies on infertility draw data from fertility clinics, which are frequented by the patients who can afford to access them, white, upper-middle class women are overrepresented in the academic discussion of infertility as well as the one in popular culture. This is not just a question of the collective imagination: it also limits much-needed investigations into conditions that are specific to marginalized demographics. For example, the treatment of fertility-impairing fibroids, which Black women experience at significantly high rates, and are still under-researched compared with conditions that are more commonly diagnosed in white women, such as endometriosis.

In March 2018, a Liberal MP, Anthony Housefather, introduced a bill that would decriminalize paying for donor eggs, sperm, and surrogacy in Canada, bringing us in line with US states where third-party reproduction is legally commercialized. The decision was met with support from infertility advocates and the LGBTQ community—and scathing op-eds by some feminist academics and journalists who were concerned that lifting the payment ban would commodify women's body parts and lead to their exploitation.

Since then, I have read dozens of accounts of surrogacy as womb renting, as animal husbandry, as slavery (whatever issues I have with these writers, I can't deny them their flair with metaphor), all of which take for granted the noncapacity of the surrogate to freely consent. A documentary about surrogacy as baby buying permanently screens on Amazon Prime Video, while a non-peer-reviewed study about the harms of donor-sperm conception on children was covered approvingly on Slate and NPR. And the sentiments survive in a diluted, everyday form, like the self-described feminist in a parenting group I joined who proclaimed that it was gestation that made one a mother.

When I read this work, I feel disoriented. If anyone was an expert on female infertility, surely it was me—at thirty-nine, I'd spent five years trying, and failing, to have a child. I'd racked up almost every diagnosis in the book, seen half a dozen specialists, and had five surgeries. I recognize nothing of this experience in the feminist debates around reproductive technology. It's the tone of them: the bloodless, objective, anthropological approach to the question of me and what to do about the problem that is me. It says something—though I'm not sure what—that I never felt the insult of being objectified as a woman more keenly than when I was infertile and reading feminist analyses of infertility: in framing infertile women as problematic consumers of technology that they despise, many contemporary feminists ignore the actual experience, the meat and pain, of infertility. They ignore the grief.

Her emotional and existential experience erased, the infertile woman first enters the public imagination not as a woman, not even as a patient, but as a consumer of biotechnology. A specific kind of consumer: the consumer as spectacle. With her grief reduced to a vague "desire" for a baby, and the efforts of making this baby rendered as so extraordinary, so risky and costly and scientifically improbable, it's difficult to see her as anything other than a curiosity of capitalism, akin to people who undergo cosmetic surgery.

"You really wanted a baby," people who have had no trouble conceiving sometimes say to me, thinking themselves supportive, affirming. And while I've tried many times to pinpoint why this offends me, there's an element I always have trouble explaining. It's not that it's trivializing; it's not that they have underestimated my grief. Rather, it's that they don't get the particular nature of this grief, how it's less about the loss of a potential child than it is about the endless possibility that there may yet be an actual child. The next procedure might work, the fallopian tube could always clear, the next fetus might not miscarry. As per the saying: miracles happen.

In my digital infertility groups, a meme is often posted beneath stories of the poorest prognoses: an image of a dandelion or a rainbow, below which is written, in cursive font: Always Hope. "I fucking hate hope," a friend who struggled with infertility before having her daughter told me recently. "Hope is how you tell women to shut up. Hope is weaponized." It's not that motherhood is out of reach, it's that it's just out of reach. It's not that motherhood didn't happen, it's that it almost did, and, in fact, still could. The difference between the grief of infertility and other forms of mourning is in that promise of "just," in "almost," in "still could." This does not make it more or less livable than other forms of grief, but it goes a long way toward explaining why it is expressed in ways that seem so desperate and even alien to the casual onlooker, why a woman might put herself under the knife ten, twelve, twenty times to get pregnant, why she might spend hundreds of thousands of dollars in the effort. The end to her grief is just so near. The tragedy of infertility is the tragedy of proximity.

Jeremy and I met the woman who would give birth to our son in January: bleak weather, waning hope. For almost five years, we had been on what insiders call a "surrogacy journey." Our first and then our second surrogates miscarried our three remaining embryos in turn before deciding not to continue. Around the same time, I had an ectopic pregnancy that required surgery. My infertility felt less like the absence of something than like a malignancy spreading from one part of my body to the next, from me to these other women who had tried to help.

In my panic, I had emailed a number of family members and friends, asking if they knew anyone who could help. It was a desperate email and one I'd sent many times to no avail. But then, as I was fear-googling surrogacy expenses, a message popped up from an address I didn't recognize. It was from a woman named Mindy who worked in college admin with my cousin and had posted about her desire to be a surrogate on Facebook. She'd been thinking about it since she and her husband had had their first child the previous year. "Having Charlotte was one of the most important things I've done," she wrote. "I really want to help someone who can't ... experience that for themselves."

When Jeremy and I met Mindy and her husband, Eric, we felt not only a rush of relief at how kind and trustworthy they seemed but also a shock of familiarity at their dynamics: their dark-humoured banter, their love of animals, the fact that they'd named their daughter Charlotte Elizabeth—the name Jeremy and I had for years on our list of names for girls. As the four of us sat in their living room and agreed to go forward, Charlotte popped up and down over the edge of her playpen, peering at me, like a tiny firecracker with pigtails shooting straight up from her head.

By the fall, Jeremy and I had nine frozen embryos—we also found Anna, our egg donor, online—but, eager as we were, the gravity of the situation hadn't fully impressed itself on me. Jeremy, Mindy, Eric, and I slogged through the routine of clearing medical, legal, and psychological screening and then the wrenching process of thawing the best embryo and, after Mindy had undergone a trying regime of injections and monitoring, transferring it to her uterus. It worked on the first try. But as the pregnancy went on, each blood test promising, each series of heartbeats measured and deemed perfect in frequency and strength, I had to accept something multiple losses had made seem impossible: we were having a baby. In gaps in my days, I found myself saying this to myself silently, over and over, like a mantra: we're having a baby. But there wasn't excitement, just relief that he was still alive, that this one wasn't dead yet. And as long as he was alive, I would not have to keep trying for him. Waiting for my baby felt less like anticipation than a break from prolonged effort and pain.

Mindy narrated what I couldn't feel: he kicked a lot, mostly at night, and he moved around when he heard music or when she'd play Jeremy's and my voices for him using headphones she'd stick on her belly. Every visit, the baby was more and more present, pushing Mindy's belly out the front of her parka, making it difficult for her to sit or run. But despite these signs of life, he was still mostly a theory, an idea. The baby that hadn't died yet.

Since he's still alive, maybe I can start buying things, I rationalized when he was still a few months away. I bought onesies with prints of ponies and hamburgers and a big, soft toy bunny, because years ago, in a dream, I'd seen a little curly-haired boy holding one. I put the things in the Room, the room that every infertile couple has, the one that is supposed to be for a baby, then fills with sad junk, until (if) luck changes. I moved around some of the junk and spread out the new cute things. But it still didn't look like stuff for a real baby in a room for a person that would actually exist. It felt provisional—stuff for a baby that hadn't died yet.

A familiar pattern of anxiety for an infertile parent-to-be, but luckily the baby himself would have none of it. He came five weeks early, quick as a flash flood, before Mindy's epidural had a chance to work and while Jeremy was in line at a Walmart, hurriedly buying a car seat.

I had spent years lamenting how invisible I felt in my infertility, how little understood, but in truth, no one would ever be more indifferent to my neuroses than my newly born son. No one cares less about your trauma than a baby does. But how quickly he eclipsed it, and us, and everything else. He changed so much in those first few minutes: at first, just a head between Mindy's thighs, then a wiggling eel, yellowish, laid down on her belly. Then, wiped down, a squalling red silhouette with a rubbery cord I cut myself and the doctor clamped with a plastic clip. Then a series of measurements—six pounds! Twenty inches!—that the doctor shouted into the room from the tiny basin in which the newborn was prodded and measured. The room collectively sighed: despite being born premature, he was healthy and robust. Then, finally, an actual, physical baby in a diaper a nurse laid between my bare chest and my hospital gown.

Apparently I was crying so hard I could barely stand; I don't remember that. What I remember is the screaming red child, the way the exact pitch of his voice had an immediate and indescribable meaning to me, the way he plugged into my chest in a very exact and deliberate way and instantly fell asleep. Eventually, Mindy turned her head and we caught each other's eye. Oh, I thought. This is what she wanted me to have. This is what she was talking about. The fact of this—that there was so great a feeling I had not known and that another woman had been willing to give it to me—overwhelmed me as much as Charlie's existence.

A common objection to surrogacy (as well as to labouring with the help of epidurals) is that it separates motherhood from the bodily work of pregnancy and childbirth. I already knew this was bullshit. The medical experience of my infertility—all the miscarriages, surgeries, tests, and IVF, as well as the physical burden of the attendant grief—was as much a part of the process of conceiving Charlie as Anna's egg retrieval or Mindy's pregnancy. I was less prepared for how bodily early motherhood was, how the combination of fatigue and a newborn baby would produce an effect that was hormonal, almost postpartum. My stomach cramped; I was sweating buckets.

Most surprisingly, my breasts were sore. Curious, I let Charlie latch and suckle and immediately felt milk pull down to my nipple. The nurse told me that, having been pregnant multiple times, I already had the plumbing to produce breast milk, and now my body was responding to the proximity of a baby. Jeremy, too, got folded into this biome, a constant, three-person exchange of touch and skin and hormone-steeped sweat; soon, we all smelled the same, like slightly sour breast milk. I did not need to go through labour to learn, as all new mothers do, that the term labour is an insulting misnomer that implies it begins with your first contraction and ends after birth.

Some people say the condition of modern womanhood is one of navigating contradictions and clashes: between the personal and the political, the said and the done, the body and the heart. For me, every time I saw Mindy, or Charlie, or even Jeremy, and every time I texted with Anna, I was aware of two stories: the one in which I had to have other women help make my baby (how sad!) and the one in which I got to have a baby with other women (pretty cool!).

A few weeks after Charlie was born, I found myself going back to my old IVF and surrogacy message boards, wondering what these communities of women could have been like in a different world. If earlier feminists had seen us as sisters rather than patriarchal dupes or oppressors of other women. If infertility lobby groups had embraced an idea of infertility as an issue of medical, emotional, and spiritual health rather than a type of consumer identity. I imagined a feminist movement parallel to the one for abortion access, in which women would call for more research into the causes of infertility, the potential efficacies and risks of various treatments.

We could call for expanded access to proven reproductive healthcare for all Canadians—not just the rich ones, not just those in cities who are partnered and straight—by demanding it be brought under the auspices of a properly regulated healthcare system. We could align ourselves with, rather than against, surrogates and egg donors in lobbying for a system in which policies around third-party reproduction are shaped by them, for their own safety and interests, which opens up the possibility of them organizing as workers. We could support infertile women who do not conceive in either finding other forms of family or healing into satisfying lives lived without children. Truly patient-centric clinics could bloom under our watch.

Perhaps most importantly, infertile feminists could embrace our status as different kinds of women—as the kinds of women who eat people in folk tales—to challenge the idea that motherhood is unthinking, automatic, and instinctual, instead of a thing that is both worked at and worked for.

THE LIFE-CHANGING MAGIC OF MAKING DO

Benjamin Leszcz

Several years ago, while living in London, England, my wife met Prince Charles at an event associated with the Prince's Foundation, where she worked. She returned with two observations: First, the Prince of Wales used two fingers—index and middle—when he pointed. Second, Charles's suit had visible signs of mending. A Google search fails to substantiate the double-barrelled gesture, but the Prince's penchant for patching has been well documented. Last year, the journalist Marion Hume discovered a cardboard box containing more than thirty years of off-cuts and leftover materials from the Prince's suits, tucked away in a corner at his Savile Row tailor, Anderson & Sheppard. "I have always believed in trying to keep as many of my clothes and shoes going for as long as possible . . . through patches and repairs," he told Ms Hume. "In this way, I tend to be in fashion once every twenty-five years."

As it happens, double-breasted suits are rather on-trend. But more notable is Charles's sartorial philosophy, which could not be timelier. The Prince comes from a tradition of admirable frugality—the Queen reuses gift-wrap—but his inclination to repair rather than replace, to wear his clothes until they wear out, is an apt antidote to our increasingly disposable times. Most modern consumers are not nearly so resourceful: the average Canadian buys seventy new pieces of clothing each year, about sixty of which ultimately wind up in a landfill. (Thrift stores only sell one in four pieces of donated clothing.) According to a British study, the average article of women's clothing is worn seven times before it's discarded.

Our bloated culture of consumption extends far beyond clothing. Each year, Canadian adults spend about $9,000 for consumer packaged goods—about twice as much as twenty-five years ago. We replace our smartphones every twenty-five months. We swap out TVs like toothbrushes. We browse for Instant Pots, pet-hair-removal gloves, and spa bath pillows when we're at dinner, when we're driving, and when we're drunk. Shopping isn't just convenient; it's inescapable. The shiny and new is seldom more than a click and a day away.

Unsurprisingly, we are drowning in stuff. Despite the average Canadian home doubling in size over the past generation—and family size shrinking—the self-storage industry is booming, with nearly three thousand jam-packed facilities nationwide. And that's just the stuff we keep: landfills are overflowing. China has stopped taking much of our recycling. Africa is refusing our used clothing. The Great Pacific Garbage Patch is one-and-a-half times the size of Ontario—and growing. Worse yet, we are spending money we don't have: the average Canadian has about $30,000 of non-mortgage debt. Ralph Waldo Emerson put it best: "Things are in the saddle, And ride mankind."

We are increasingly desperate for a way out. For many, salvation has come via Marie Kondo, author of *The Life-Changing Magic of Tidying Up*. Ms Kondo's KonMari method centres on a now-famous question: Does this thing I own spark joy for me? If not, it is to be discarded. Others have found emancipation via such figures as Leo Babauta, Dave Bruno, and Tammy Strobel, avowed minimalists who own fifty, one hundred, and seventy-two things, respectively.

It is easy to understand the appeal of these alternative ideologies of consumerism, both of which reflect the same fundamental truth: All this stuff isn't making us happy. Minimalism is simple but extreme; KonMari has broader appeal, promising a more fulfilling relationship with things, once we've purged ourselves of the non-joy-producing inventory. But KonMari asks both far too much of our things, and not nearly enough. When Prince Charles opens his closet, surely he does not ask if his fine double-breasted suit sparks joy. Instead, he asks: "Does this fine double-breasted suit fulfill my need for today, which is to wear a fine double-breasted suit while pointing at my subjects with two fingers?" It is a profoundly simple question, the spirit of which has been lost entirely today. In asking this question, Charles affirms his position as an unlikely champion for the forgotten virtue of making do.

Making do is a deeply pragmatic philosophy. It means asking of our things the only question we should ever ask of them: "Can you fulfill your intended use for me?" The answer—if we can be honest, and resist a moment of discomfort, inconvenience or boredom—is, extraordinarily often, yes. Making do is about taming the reflex to discard, replace, or upgrade; it's about using things well, and using them until they are used up. Taken literally, it simply means making something perform—making it do what it ought to do.

If Marie Kondo delights in discarding, making do is about agonizing over it, admitting that we probably should not have bought that thing in the first place. Instead of thanking our outgoing goods for their meagre service, per Ms Kondo, making do means admonishing ourselves for being so thoughtless in the first place. Ditching something costs us, ecologically and cosmically; it should sting. And it should teach us to think more carefully about the real value of things.

As Juliet Schor writes in *Plenitude: The New Economics of True Wealth*, "We don't need to be less materialistic, as the standard formulation would have it, but more so." By becoming more materialistic, in this deeper sense, we can radically reorient our relationship with things. In this way, we can not only mitigate the high cost of thoughtless consumption, saving us money and the planet harm, but also, we might just wind up a whole lot happier.

Making do, in times of scarcity, is straightforward: If our weekly sugar ration is two hundred grams, then we get by. In the context of abundance, it's complicated. How do we set limits when more, or new, is easily within reach?

The challenge, of course, is that making do is at odds with human nature. As products of evolution, we are predisposed to seek novelty, variety, and excess; now, we hunt for bargains, not mastodons. Even Adam Smith, the forefather of homo economicus—that perfectly rational, utility-seeking consumer of classical economics—wrote in *The Theory of Moral Sentiments* in 1759 that "frivolous objects ... [are] often the secret motive of the most serious and important pursuits."

In other words, to be frivolous is to be human. To aspire to pure pragmatism—to own only necessities—is misguided. "The fundamental question of what is essential and what is not has been a moving target, at least since the fifteenth century," says Frank Trentmann, author of *Empire of Things: How We Became a World of Consumers*. "Every generation complains that the lower orders are suddenly wanting things that their parents or grandparents didn't have." Making do accommodates for this kind of hedonic adaptation; it allows for wide-ranging materialism, provided it is thoughtful, critical, and honest.

For me, making do is an aspiration; I often fall short. I succeeded, however, with my previous television, an off-brand, early-generation flatscreen. Friends mocked me, but in an era in which we happily watch three-inch screens, I deemed my twelve-year-old Olevia adequate. (My company recently replaced its boardroom TV; I took the cast-off home, and gave the Olevia to a friend.) It was a small but meaningful victory, especially for household appliances, which tend to visit our homes briefly en route to the landfill.

As a parent, in an era in which toy companies have stretched commercials to twenty-two-minute-long episodes, temptation is everywhere. Still, I'm a hardcore proponent of the cardboard-box theory of toys (the box—and later, the unboxing—trumps the contents). I virtually never buy toys. When my kids ask, I say, "We don't really buy stuff like that." (My eldest is five; wish me luck.)

My wife rejected my pitch for our kids to wear potato sacks until the age of twelve, presumably because most potato sacks are paper nowadays. Still, we opt for hand-me-downs or second-hand where possible. And we supplement with fast fashion, seeking clothes that last, at least, until they cease to fit anyone in our home.

As grown-ups, however, our relationship with clothing is perhaps the most unhinged. The novelist Ann Patchett, in her terrific *New York Times* column about giving up shopping for a year, recounts interviewing Tom Hanks before a large audience: "Previously, I would have believed that such an occasion demanded a new dress and lost two days of my life looking for one. In fact, Tom Hanks had never seen any of my dresses, nor had the people in the audience. I went to my closet, picked out something weather appropriate and stuck it in my suitcase. Done."

By disavowing shopping, Ms Patchett embraced the spirit of making do. Had she snagged that dress on a nail that evening, she could have made do on an even higher level. Getting the most out of things often requires investment, and the economics of repair can be challenging: It may be cheaper to buy a new sweater, made in Bangladesh, than to pay a Canadian tailor to fix an old one. Ideally, we'd mend it ourselves—a basic repertoire of DIY repair skills is wonderful way to make do—

but either way, there's deep value in reviving the thing. Never mind that a mended garment is perfectly functional; it's often improved, imbued with a hint of effortless imperfection.

Worn clothing can be a marker of status in its own right, as it is for *The Bonfire of the Vanities*' Sherman McCoy. Tom Wolfe describes the Master of the Universe's "worn but formidable rubberized British riding mac … after the fashion of the Boston Cracked Shoe look." (The look references the habit, traditional among New England patricians, of wearing well-cared-for but dramatically aged shoes.) To certain elites, then, making do is familiar as a style if not an ethos. *The Official Preppy Handbook* advises, "Never replace anything until you have exhausted all possibility of repair, restoration or rehabilitation. No matter what it is, they don't make it as well as they used to." The key to a making-do revolution, of course, would be for the style to sweep the country. "I've always thought, there may come a point where the way to distinguish yourself and signal status is precisely by getting away from this increasing acceleration of consumption," Mr Trentmann says. "To stand out because you drive an old car."

Until that day comes, getting mileage from our things should at least engender a sense of pride, and of mastery. This is a more difficult proposition with electronics, appliances, and cars, for which technology has largely rendered repairs of any kind impossible. Still, making do means making an effort to preserve or repair, and spending more than simple economics might justify.

The corollary here is that making do means avoiding in the first place products that aren't worth repairing. The problem of durability preoccupies Dieter Rams, the designer of Braun's most iconic mid-century products. Mr Ram's mantra is "less, but better," and in the recent documentary about his career, he rails against "thoughtless design and thoughtless consumption." For Mr Rams, it is incumbent on designers to make products that endure. (It's a cruel irony that Apple, whose product design owes so much to Mr Rams, has become a paragon of built-in obsolescence.)

Byron and Dexter Peart, who made their names as fashion-accessory designers, are following Mr Rams with Goodee, an online marketplace of ethically produced housewares. Goodee products "are meant to be used everyday and passed down for generations," the twin Peart brothers say. "For products to be essential, they must be designed with rigour and built to last, both from a standpoint of quality manufacturing, as well as a timeless aesthetic."

Many fashion brands lure customers with the promise of enduring essentials, from the luxury house Bottega Veneta (former creative director Tomas Maier: "I want to own one suit") to the women's-wear line Cuyana ("Welcome to fewer, better things"). Luxury watches do it, too: "You never actually own a Patek Philippe. You merely look after it for the next generation." (Though my $50 Timex keeps on ticking, too.) Of course, for people with the means, places such as Anderson & Sheppard, or the shoemaker Church's, perform miraculous repairs as a matter of course. Roche Bobois and Stickley make furniture that retains its value—if it doesn't appreciate. Making do can mean embracing luxury, transforming our conception of heirlooms from relics of the past to ambitions for the future. But it also means patronizing more accessible brands such as LL Bean, Filson, Barbour, Patagonia, Arc'teryx, and The North Face, all of which repair their goods, and some of which buy back, refurbish, and resell worn garments. Even more accessible is Uniqlo, whose unadorned designs eschew trends (and whose $30 oxford-cloth dress shirts are my uniform of choice). In *The Atlantic* this year, Gillian B White wrote, "in an era of disposable fashion, a Uniqlo garment, made from hearty materials and cut in a timeless style, can feel like an investment piece." It's an overstatement—my shirts, at least, depreciate steadily—but it underscores the role of design in reshaping consumption.

Another key to making do is scratching our acquisitive itch in creative ways. Thanks to my kids, I have become reacquainted with the Toronto Public Library, where I can indulge my impulse to acquire books I think I'll read. (Typically by the third renewal, my deluded literary ambitions dissipate.) Following Rent the Runway, scores of clothing-rental services are launching, from mass brands such as Express to local startups such as STMNT, which was founded by a pair of Western University grads. Even IKEA is launching a rental program in thirty countries. Purchases—like tattoos—are permanent decisions based on temporary feelings; renting, or borrowing, is often a better response.

As we become increasingly dismayed by our limitless consumption, positive alternatives abound. But too often, alternative modes of consumption simply become additional modes of consumption. In pursuit of fewer, better, we sometimes end up with more, more. Of course, Mr Rams is correct: Disposability is a design problem. But more than that, it is a psychology problem. Making do has a societal scope, but it is a profoundly personal project.

In the final pages of *The Life-Changing Magic of Tidying Up*, Ms Kondo writes, "I can think of no greater happiness in life than to be surrounded only by the things I love." It is a powerful statement, entirely on-brand for Ms Kondo. It's also a bleak reflection of how distracted our stuff makes us from the things that actually make us happy: a sense of belonging, of community, of purpose. Time with family and friends. Great books. Long meals. We know all this, and yet: we are living amidst an unprecedented epidemic of loneliness, experiencing friendships through Instagram; consuming culture through Netflix; and walking alone through our neighbourhoods, AirPods in place, our faces illuminated by Amazon's frictionless mobile-shopping experience. We are isolated and unmoored. And with nothing to tell us who we are, we shop and shop and shop, filling our carts when we really just want to fill our lives.

Laurie Santos, who created Yale University's most popular course, "Psychology and the Good Life," often says, "Our intuitions about what to do to be happy are wrong." This simple truth is at the heart of making do, which emphatically reminds us that our things will never make us happy. Our things are a healthy, normal, inevitable part of life, but in the end, they are just things. By asking of them only what they can give us—not love, or joy, or a sense of purpose or connection—we are far more likely to get it. That doesn't guarantee happiness, but it clears the path, highlighting an essential, unmissable truth: The stuff of life isn't stuff at all.

THE DISNEYLAND OF DEATH

Larissa Diakiw

I took the bus to Forest Lawn Memorial Park after waking up on a blow-up mattress in my friend's tiny Koreatown apartment. I had fallen asleep to the sound of a pastor preaching in Spanish at the storefront church across the street, my first Los Angeles lullaby. His voice was distorted by a loudspeaker and had a soothing evangelical lilt. I drank tea, which I wished was coffee. I wrote down the directions via public transit to the cemetery on a piece of paper, in case my phone died. I didn't want to get lost in the chaotic outskirts.

Forest Lawn is a cemetery in Glendale just north of LA. It has been described as a Disneyland of Death and a theme-park necropolis. It has been satirized by Evelyn Waugh, depicted by Aldous Huxley. Stars and moguls from Hollywood's golden era are buried in its hilltop terraces. It created a new template for death culture in North America, and a business model for other cemeteries to follow.

From the bus window, I watched hairy palms rise in lonely spikes along the street. Morning smog gave the city a haunted look. The exotic cut leaves and absurd shag of the palms appeared from the mist like an idea of a place. We passed through Chinatown, where a group of old men and women, bent over trundle-buggies, stood waiting in line. When the bus stopped, they slowly filed on, helping one another up the steps, around the corner, into a seat. A woman with silver hair tied in a French-roll sat next to me and asked where I was going. Glendale, I said. She said she had made the trek downtown to get food for the week, but it was difficult to carry anything, let alone the six bags she was struggling with. I asked why she didn't use a buggy like the others. Her daughter wouldn't let her, she said, because it made her look old.

What do cemeteries say about the living, those left to grieve a future that had once included the dead? What do these placeless places say about the cultures that create them? In the introduction to *The Work of the Dead*, Thomas Laqueur asks why the dead matter. Why does a culture of care for the dead extend across time, across landscapes, across different systems of belief, even to those who don't believe? There is evidence of Neanderthal burials in French caves, and Laqueur describes atheists leaving mementos on graves with wonder. It is interesting, he notes, that without a system of ritual, without belief in an afterlife, uncared-for remains are still somehow culturally unbearable. The idea that a body would be left to rot, bones exposed, seems like an act of violence. But why does it matter? "It matters," he writes, "because the living need the dead far more than the dead need the living. It matters because we cannot bear to live at the borders of our mortality."

The founding myth of Forest Lawn has Hubert Eaton standing on a hilltop in 1912 looking down at brown fields of devil grass, wild oat sprouting at random between broken tombstones, maybe a tumbleweed blowing past his feet, and there and then he decides to take on a job as manager of the desolate graveyard. In his mind's eye he can already see the pastoral garden he will build, "Filled with Towering Trees, Sweeping Lawns, Splashing Fountains, Singing Birds." In the same way that middle-class desire dreamed up suburbia, a place where everyone has their own patch of lawn to fortify their bungalows against real wilderness, carpets of sod would be unrolled and laid across the hills, smothering the chaparral in an act of botanical colonialism. That night, so the myth goes, Eaton stayed awake writing the "Builder's Creed" in a hotel room where he detailed his vision for a new way of dealing with death. This manifesto is carved into a stone tablet and displayed on the grounds. Two alabaster sculptures of children holding hands, a puppy curled beside them, look up at it. Copies are available at the gift shop. "I BELIEVE IN A HAPPY ETERNAL LIFE," it starts. It isn't only immortality that serves as a constitutional concept here but unchecked joy. This sentiment is key to understanding the modern American memorial park. Happiness is built into every aspect of the design. When Eaton vows to create a cemetery "As unlike other cemeteries as sunshine is to darkness, as eternal life is unlike death..." he creates a cemetery in denial, a place that banishes any sign of decay, where grief is forbidden, where pain is repressed, where no one dies.

Tombstones were removed, because Eaton felt they were too morose, and replaced with brass plaques. No new deciduous trees would be planted, because their leafless branches in winter reminded him of death. The evergreens, alternatively, were symbols of everlasting life, and planted in swaths across the property.

Forest Lawn is three hundred acres of emerald green hills enclosed by a wrought iron fence. Walls and fences are a classic feature of historical European cemeteries. They have practical applications, like keeping animals in or out, but symbolically, they define the boundaries between opposing worlds. When you step into a cemetery, leaving everyday life, strip malls and highways, taco stands and nail salons, you enter a different territory, an unstable one, a supernatural one. Somehow the cemetery is a permeable place, shared by the dead and the living, where ghosts might glimmer at night like electric filaments on the hills. Forest Lawn doesn't feel spooky. It looks like a well-manicured park, with fields and fields of brass plaques that disappear into the endless grass depending on your vantage point. It is a place where someone might go for a morning run with a dalmatian at their heels.

I walked ten minutes from the bus stop to the gate. The road in leads past a fountain and duck pond, to an empty parking lot. Canadian geese linger near the water. The entire place has a monumental scale meant to impress and dwarf the visitor. When I finally got to the crest of the hill, after walking for forty-five minutes through football field after football field, past curbs with the names of burial plots stamped into the concrete, Slumberland, Lullaby Land, Dawn of Tomorrow, Vesperland, I drank some water and found myself on a bench in a courtyard fatuously named the Garden of the Mystery of Life. The bench was in a niche, surrounded by boxwood hedges. Azaleas were in bloom nearby. From that height I could see Babyland, a plot reserved for children, at the bottom of the hill, circled by a heart-shaped road. I could see Glendale past the cemetery walls, buildings pale under the stark sun, spilling into the valley below.

Looking at aerial photos of fault lines in the desert is a strange and beautiful thing. From above they resemble sutures, or healed scars. As if the ground itself is trying to close over an old wound. Glendale is where the San Fernando and San Gabriel valleys meet. Subterranean fault lines crisscross underneath the city. Not too far north, the San Andreas fault readies for the next imminent tectonic shift, estimated to happen anytime between tomorrow and the next decade.

The politics of water in the desert are always fierce. LA drained Owens Valley by 1926 in order to quench its thirst. During the last drought, some Californian landscapers started painting their client's dormant grass green in order not to be shamed. To make a paradise grow in a semi-arid state, massive amounts of water are needed. In 1985 the Los Angeles

Times reported that Forest Lawn's then 125 acres of grass, 10,000 trees, and 100,000 shrubs required an estimated 195 million gallons of water a year. The City of Glendale negotiated a deal where the cemetery would use recycled water rather than potable water, promising to supply 200 million gallons per year for twenty years, and help in the construction of a pipeline to deliver the water from a treatment plant to the cemetery. It takes a lot of water to create an oasis in a desert.

Glendale is in a chaparral ecosystem. It should be a landscape of coastal sage, drought-tolerant yucca with pillars of dead flowers, silvery artemisia, oak savannas, thickets of heathland, wildflowers. The cycle of the chaparral requires regular forest fires. Some plants need heat, smoke, or changes to the chemical composition of the soil to germinate. Some plants, called fire followers, like phacelia, need the extra light after a canopy is burnt to grow. If you have seen phacelia it would be hard to argue it isn't magical. Iridescent blue whiskers poke out from clusters of bell-shaped flowers on a spiral stem. I have only seen photos. But these plants don't fit into the nostalgic image of an imagined garden, a hegemonic Eden. California does not have the same climate as Cambridge or Milan. What did Eaton know about the ecology of the land he was building on? And where did he get his version of paradise?

I like to visit cemeteries when I travel. In Guadalajara, loved ones' initials are scratched into the flesh of the cacti that define the boundaries of the grounds. In Salem, every tombstone has hand-carved Puritan poetry under a winged skull. Erosion has almost erased the words, and to read the verse, you trace your fingers across the stone, pretending it's braille. In some areas of Istanbul marble tombstones spill between buildings, or in courtyards of homes. In Montreal, tiny mausoleums in the centre of Mount Royal house artifacts of past lives like baseball bats, and daguerreotypes are permanently affixed to granite tombstones so visitors can look directly into the past.

Cemeteries are like love letters to the dead. They say so much about the culture that cares for and creates them.

It was difficult for me to understand what created this place, sitting on a bench next to delicately pruned topiary, a replica of Michelangelo's *David* looming larger than life from the next courtyard. His marble face eyed the hills as though X-ray vision allowed him to see skeletons under the surface of sod. But that is David before he fought Goliath, tense. A vein bulges in his neck. He readies for the fight, slingshot over his shoulder. During the earthquake in 1971 he fell off his stand and smashed to pieces. He was quickly replaced, that time without a fig leaf, then taken down after a group of concerned citizens complained about the full frontal. Now he guards the graves of Mary Pickford and Humphrey Bogart without shame.

The architecture and sculpture scattered across the grounds is a mishmash of classical European histories. There is a Tudor mortuary. Three churches on the grounds are copied from originals in Scotland and Ireland. The Great Mausoleum is based on Campo Santo in Genoa. There is a stained-glass recreation of Leonardo's *Last Supper*, and a cast of Michelangelo's version of *La Pietà*. The sculpture where Mary cradles Jesus in her arms after the crucifixion. Something feels absent in these bleached recreations. The patina of age is missing. I can imagine Eaton and his team picking and choosing status symbols to fluff up the place, without any consideration of the original meaning behind the art. They seem gaudy in their perfection, insincere, out of place. This paradise is a transplant from someone else's past.

Forest Lawn has been an important part of American death culture since it opened, influencing and changing how we mourn. Jessica Mitford dedicates an entire chapter to the cemetery and its management in her book *The American Way of Death*. Originally published in 1962, reprinted with an update in 1998, Mitford investigates how the funeral industry is embedded in entrepreneurial capitalism, detailing some of its sleazy money-making tactics. She describes how embalming is explained as a hygiene issue to grieving families, expensive and nearly non-negotiable. The World Health Organization does not agree that embalming plays any role in decreasing the spread of disease, though Mitford was led to believe by various funeral directors at the time of her reporting that it was legally required. Similarly, expensive cement vaults were said to be legally necessary so that the ground didn't cave in, though that was also untrue.

Mitford describes Eaton as a sort of megalomaniac, and the loudspeakers that used to dot the property, reminding visitors to visit the gift shop between musical interludes, as another dark money grab. Forest Lawn management set a precedent with sales tactics and strategies to exploit the bereaved. Euphemism becomes key to sales, cloaking meaning. If you avoid calling up context or images and instead use words that are so general, so vague, they mean almost nothing, whatever you are describing remains unreal. An entire language was codified, a language that is still used. Funeral directors are instructed not to say hearse but casket-coach. They don't say grave, they say interment space. They don't say dirt, they say earth. They don't say cemetery, they say memorial park. They don't say dead body, they say mortal remains. They don't say died, they say passed on. It is easier to up-sell a casket than a coffin. The entire cemetery relies on this distance from the facts, ushering in a new era of mourning. One where every American family should employ a cosmetician to paint lifeless faces so they might look alive again. Prices are inflated. Unusual costs stack up. And Forest Lawn is a gleaming example of cemetery as business.

As I was walking along a winding road towards the Great Mausoleum, thinking of celebrity, a memory came to me.

When Patrick Swayze died in 2009, I visited someone in the intensive care unit at a psych ward. My friend in the hospital described her psychosis to me while we sat in plastic chairs around a wooden table. She said she was seeing faces in her food. As she spoke, she flipped between euphoria and terror. Tears rolled down her face. She told me she had been chosen. In my memory she stood up as she said this, put her open palms down, and looked across the table with such a profound longing, I will never forget it. On my way out, I crossed the path of one skeletal patient walking up and down the hallway, repeating the same rigid gestures of kneeling and opening his mouth to take eucharist. Down on his knees an invisible priest would place the wafer on his tongue. He would get up and start again, locked in a perpetual cycle of atonement. Another patient bounced on the balls of his feet and promised to skin a squirrel next time I visited. It was easy, he said, you just have to catch one.

A doctor once described brains in trauma or psychosis to me as crushed rubber balls that need time to return to their original form. The more often they are crushed the more difficult it is for them to get back to the previous shape. I wonder if this is an appropriate metaphor for someone who isn't a clinician. What I am left with is the simpler understanding that psychosis or mania are traumatic and require healing. After I left the hospital that day, I stopped for tea at a friend's house in Pointe-Saint-Charles. We were talking about this idea of healing when a downstairs neighbour pounded up the stairs and stormed into the room, shouting that Patrick Swayze had died. We put down our tea. The neighbour was crying. What was there to say? We went silent. It wasn't an ideal moment for us to offer comfort. I thought about the actor, as the neighbour continued screaming, and felt nothing. I couldn't understand where her pain was coming from. "What the fuck do I care?" I said, "Everyone dies." Anger inhabited my body. I saw the hospital room in my mind, the colour of the walls. But she cared.

"What about the people you actually know?" I said. It wasn't that I disliked Patrick Swayze. But why was she weeping for him? Why did she care more for him? She had funnelled all her emotion onto a stranger, an idea of a person, when people we knew were in the hospital. I couldn't understand.

Mourning the death of the famous is not a new cultural phenomenon. When Victor Hugo died two million people joined his funeral procession. Even more showed up to mourn Ayatollah Khomeini. His is in the running for largest funeral in history. The Egyptian singer Umm Kulthum, and Evita Perón, had millions pass by their dead bodies to show respect. When Prince died, the internet collectively mourned and celebrated him. "Purple Rain" played all summer in bars and coffee shops. I was in El Salvador when Shafik Handal, the leader of the FMLN party and former guerilla, died in 2006. I was in a small inland village, though nothing is very far from the ocean in El Salvador. The woman I was staying with, Fidelina, carted me and her entire family of nine onto a bus to go view the body in San Salvador. We waited in line for hours to have our turn to look at his open casket. The crowd was a sea of FMLN-red baseball caps and shirts, moving slowly, mournfully. Fidelina wiped her eyes with a handkerchief she kept in her bra. I had never seen a dead body before. I wasn't sure what to expect after an embalmer and cosmetician had been at work. When our turn came, we were each given a private moment to look at the body, a confirmation, a recognition, thirty seconds. The casket was on stage in an auditorium that reminded me of the wooden stage of my high school. Shafik's face in my memory was blue, strained, doll-like. He was dressed in military regalia, epaulettes, medals. I was surprised that I wanted to linger, to be close to him. I barely knew who he was. The feeling of collective grief was powerful. When my thirty seconds were up, I was directed off stage by soldiers flanking the coffin, holding AK47s, and I wanted more time. I wasn't ready to say goodbye.

It is difficult not to ask questions about private and public grief when walking around Forest Lawn. Who has a right to mourn whom? What is the relationship between a celebrity and their fans? Or a public who has never met the person they adore? How does capital factor? Do celebrities owe nothing to their audience? What if they have transformed someone's life? Michael Jackson is interred in a sarcophagus in the Great Mausoleum. The door is locked. You cannot visit him, unless you are a family member or on a list of ten who have their own sets of keys. None of the graves are easy to find. The cemetery management dissuades tomb tourists, or death hags, or pilgrims hunting idols. They frown on the idea that non-family members want to visit a grave, but people are resilient. You can find blogs that give vague directions, but it isn't easy to find them once you are there. What is the point if only a few can mourn? The only celebrity grave I saw at Forest Lawn was Larry's, the curly haired third Stooge. A wilted rose and comic book had been left as a token, leaning against his granite plaque.

There are important people buried at Forest Lawn: Dorothy Dandridge, Sammy Davis Jr., Clark Gable, Walt Disney, Sam Cooke, Jean Harlow, Clara Bow, Nat King Cole. I try to imagine who would be compelled by these lives, and what a visit in-memoriam might mean to them. Religious impresarios of early Los Angeles spiritualism are also buried in Forest Lawn. Paramahansa Yogananda, the Indian guru who was integral in spreading yoga and meditation to the US, and who wrote the cult classic *Autobiography of a Yogi*, is in the Great Mausoleum. The evangelist Aimee Semple McPherson, who died in 1944, is buried on the grounds. She had one of the largest congregations in the city. They would watch in rapture as she mixed Hollywood-style theatrics with Pentecostal revival. She faked her own kidnapping on Venice Beach so she could hide out with a lover, was credited with countless faith healings, and was known for her ability to translate for people speaking in tongues. She once rode down the aisle of a church on a motorbike, dressed as a cop, then screeched to a stop at the pulpit and said "Stop, you're speeding towards hell." Are her followers entitled to pay homage by leaving flowers or visiting her tomb? Or was she always meant to remain separate, cloistered, and elite? Her grave is easier to find than others, but the point still stands.

Maybe a piece of the mourner's identity dies with the dead. Movies, literature, music, all factor into how we build our identities. We learn how to love, what to expect from love, what love is. This is a problem when we look at who is writing these stories, what is included and what is omitted. We may spend our lives undoing that damage, but we remain affected by different iterations of our past selves. My friend's neighbour, in her sadness over Patrick Swayze's death, may have been grieving not Swayze, but her twelve-year-old self, sitting on the carpeted floor of her parents' living room, watching movies on late-night TV in flannel pyjamas, safe before her mother died, stuffing handfuls of popcorn drenched in butter into her mouth, mesmerized. The future still possible.

In Eastern Orthodox graveyards, unbaptized babies are buried at the forest's edge, not quite in consecrated ground, not quite on the unholy other side, but in the limbo between. The Belfast city cemetery has a six-foot underground wall to separate Protestants from Catholics. Paupers' graves are shared by whoever can't pay and are left unmarked, whereas the graves nearest a church are reserved for well-paying clients or the clergy. This is a factor in understanding the landscape Eaton created. Forest Lawn was segregated for decades. I messaged the cemetery's livestream, a service offered on their website where a technician responds immediately to any questions, to ask details. What years was the Memorial Park segregated for? I wrote. The technician slowly typed out, That's a good question, but didn't know the answer, and referred me to an email address. No one responded to any of my several emails. The Supreme Court officially ruled in 1948 that racially restrictive land deeds violated the Fourteenth Amendment in Shelley v Kramer, which would eventually be applied to burial plots. Despite not getting any concrete dates from the technician, I do know that for decades Forest Lawn refused to bury anyone who was Black, Jewish, Chinese. The idea that a body can infect another body is a dark holdover from living society. Cities of the dead are bound by the same laws of hate and exploitation as cities of the living. This is what I walk through as I trudge naively up hills with my notebook in hand, histories of power. Paradise is defined by who is allowed in and who isn't. It is a site of exclusion, and the cemetery is its worldly counterpart.

The gated courtyards on the hilltops are mostly locked. Several times, when I neared a locked gate, I was approached by security, who were everywhere, and asked if I needed help. Decorum is strictly regulated and carefully policed. There is a code of conduct for mourners that they agree to when they buy a plot. No balloons, spinners, ornamentation, planters, statues, or stones are permitted on the graves. Potted flowers can be no larger than eight inches in diameter. Cut flowers will be removed in three days. No one can lie down on the grass or have a picnic. I did see a family having a meal at a graveside, a Californian ritual. They were sitting in camping chairs, eating sandwiches, and sharing a bottle of soda water among the fields and fields of brass plaques, but I imagine they were told off eventually. Signs near the road warn "flower theft is a crime punishable by imprisonment." Security guards ride around on golf carts watching you carefully, noting you as you walk, even more so at the crests of the hills, like an economic reflection of LA itself. I thought maybe I could convince someone to let me inside one of the locked courtyards, but they worked in pairs, so I didn't try. I joked about the weather to make them smile, hoping they wouldn't kick me out.

When I finally got back to the wrought-iron gates, I wasn't sure where I had been. I felt unmoved, exhausted. Forest Lawn's marketing claims the gates are the biggest of their kind in the world, ten thousand pounds, twenty-five-feet high, eighty-feet wide, larger than the gates at Buckingham Palace, or Topkapi. Laqueur suggests that the dead inhabit two distinct cultural landscapes. The graveyard, where their physical bodies or ashes are interred, and an imagined world, a shadowland without maps or clear geography, heaven, hell, purgatory, the void on the other side of the River Styx, potential and emptiness all at the same time. The graveyard offers a dangerous window onto the other side. It is important to know when you have entered and when you have left. One superstition says that, when leaving a cemetery, you should touch the iron gate, so any clinging ghosts are stopped from following you. I reach up to feel the metal as I pass. It is cold under my palm.

IN THE US CAMPUS SPEECH WARS, PALESTINIAN ADVOCACY IS A BLIND SPOT

Andy Lamey

In 2015, a group of undergraduates applied to establish Students for Justice in Palestine (SJP) as a club at Fordham University in New York City. In accordance with the school's policies, the students submitted paperwork stating that their goal was to "build support in the Fordham community among people of all ethnic and religious backgrounds for the promotion of justice, human rights, liberation and self-determination for the indigenous Palestinian people." The applicants also stated that the club would participate in the Boycott, Divestment and Sanctions (BDS) campaign against Israel. In 2016, Fordham's Dean of Education denied the club's application on the grounds that it would likely be polarizing, singling out its support for BDS. The students took Fordham to court. In August, a New York judge struck down the Dean's decision as "arbitrary and capricious."

The court's verdict was a win for the Fordham students. But the fact that setting up their club required four years and a lawsuit is telling. As the judge noted, Fordham has clear rules about creating clubs, and they don't include a requirement to avoid polarization. In invoking a new standard, the Dean was plainly discriminating against SJP.

Fordham is not alone. In recent years, pro-Palestinian students and faculty across the United States have faced barriers in seeking to exercise their rights—including bureaucratic stonewalling, punitive legal actions, and termination of employment.

These responses often are initiated by Pro-Israel groups, which seek to silence Pro-Palestinian voices by using tools ostensibly designed to counter racism. Such tools include civil-rights lawsuits; an expanded definition of anti-Semitism (one that equates legitimate criticism of the Israeli government with prejudice against Jewish people); and an outsized concern with intellectual "safety," according to which robust criticisms of Israel are said to harm Jewish students. This silencing campaign presents itself as inclusive and therapeutic. In reality, it poses a significant threat to intellectual and academic freedom, yet one that seems perennially overlooked in the campus speech wars.

The nature of that threat will be obvious to anyone sympathetic to the Palestinian cause. But the campus crackdown on Pro-Palestinian voices should also concern those with no special interest in this subject. Free inquiry is not just an intellectual value. It is also a moral one. As the political philosopher Ronald Dworkin aptly observed, "academic freedom plays an important ethical role not just in the lives of the few people it protects, but in the life of the community more generally." The more that freedom is compromised, the greater the risk of an enforced intellectual conformity, not just for wild-eyed professors with unwelcome views, but for everyone.

The Israeli operation Summer Rains marked a turning point in the history of American free speech. The 2006 military action was the first in a long-running series of clashes between Israel and the Hamas-run Gaza Strip. Summer Rains began a pattern of Israel responding to rocket fire and other violent provocations with overwhelming force. The 2014 Gaza War was perhaps the starkest example. A United Nations report found that while both sides committed war crimes, Israel killed over 2,200 Palestinians, 65 percent of whom were civilians. Of the 73 Israeli dead, all but six were soldiers.

The conflict coincided with the rise of social media. For many Palestinian supporters, its defining image was a photo of a dead Palestinian girl on a beach that was tweeted by Anthony Bourdain, and later retweeted over 14,000 times. The increasing availability of unfiltered images of Palestinian casualties sparked an upsurge in pro-Palestinian activism on US campuses—activism that has met with its own disproportionate response.

This history is documented "The Palestine Exception to Free Speech: A Movement Under Attack in the US," a 2015 report from Palestine Legal, a group that, by its own description, "protects the civil and constitutional rights of people in the US who speak out for Palestinian freedom." Their report catalogs incidents stretching back over the previous decade, and notes that threats to the intellectual freedom of pro-Palestinian groups were reported especially frequently in 2014 and the first half of 2015, a period during which Palestine Legal responded to 292 incidents of alleged censorship or punishment—as well as 101 further requests for legal assistance in anticipation of such actions. According to "The Palestine Exception," "the overwhelming majority of these incidents—89 percent in 2014 and 80 percent in the first half of 2015—targeted students and scholars, a reaction to the increasingly central role universities play in the movement for Palestinian rights."

Targeted student activism often involved chapters of SJP, such as was the case at Fordham. SJP at Northeastern University in Boston, for example, organized the distribution of mock eviction notices in a campus dormitory in 2014, which stated (falsely) that the building was scheduled for demolition. The flyers were meant to draw attention to demolitions of Palestinian dwellings, and contained a note indicating they were not actual eviction notices. The university formally suspended SPJ for this (and for previous incidents, for which SJP denied responsibility), and its members were interviewed by police. The suspension was lifted after the American Civil Liberties Union and other rights groups challenged it as viewpoint discrimination.

Beyond SJP, targeted student groups included BAKA (Belief, Awareness, Knowledge, Action) at Rutger's University's New Brunswick campus in New Jersey. In 2010, BAKA held a fundraiser to support a boat that would participate in the "Gaza Freedom Flotilla," which sought to break the Gaza blockade. The Jewish campus organization Hillel and the Anti-Defamation League (ADL) condemned the fundraising as illegal support for terrorism. Although the flotilla was advertised as a humanitarian initiative, Hillel and the ADL said that it was likely to deliver "material assistance" to Hamas, which the United States has designated a Foreign Terrorist Organization. The university prevented BAKA from donating the raised funds to the non-profit group supporting the flotilla, and ultimately redirected the money to a different charity.

In addition to listing incidents of heavy-handed responses to student activism, "The Palestine Exception" documents professors whose academic freedom has been compromised. While some examples concern Gaza specifically, many of the listed professors were carrying out research or teaching concerned with Palestinian issues more generally. Representative examples include:

Nadia Abu El-Haj, anthropologist at Barnard College in New York City. Abu El Haj wrote a 2001 book arguing that archaeological research in Israel is conducted and interpreted with the goal of supporting the country's territorial claims. In 2007, a graduate of Barnard who had settled in the West Bank launched a petition calling for Abu El-Haj's application for tenure to be denied. The petition, which attracted over 2,500 signatures, alleged that she could not read Hebrew, alongside other false claims with the potential to ruin her reputation. Abu El-Haj was granted tenure, but the resulting harassment and threats compelled her to remove her phone and office-location details from the Barnard directory.

Norman Finkelstein, political scientist at DePaul University in Chicago. Finkelstein, a polemical critic of Israel and the author of controversial books such as *The Holocaust Industry*, used harsh and insulting language to criticize the scholarship of Harvard law professor Alan Dershowitz, a prominent defender of Israel. Dershowitz subsequently "launched a national crusade to deny Finkelstein tenure," as the blog of *Academe* magazine put it. Finkelstein's 2007 tenure file was approved by his department and by a review committee, but was ultimately denied by the university, which cited his lack of "civility" toward Dershowitz and other critics. Finkelstein has subsequently held no academic appointment at any American university.

Terri Ginsberg, cinema professor at North Carolina State University. In 2007, Ginsberg held a non-tenure-track position, in which capacity she hosted a Middle East film series. Members of her department encouraged her to apply for a permanent position, and notes by members of the search committee described her as the best of the "First Tier Candidates." At a screening of *Ticket to Jerusalem*, about a Palestinian filmmaker who struggles to show a film in East Jerusalem, "Ginsberg thanked the audience for supporting the screening of alternate viewpoints such as the one in the film," according to a lawsuit she later filed against the university. It alleged that she was chastised, pressured to resign from the film series, and rejected for the permanent position. After losing her lawsuit, Ginsberg applied for 150 jobs but received no interviews. She now works at the American University of Cairo.

Kristofer Petersen-Overton, adjunct professor and PhD student at the City University of New York (CUNY). In 2010, Petersen-Overton was fired a week before he was scheduled to begin teaching a class on the politics of the Middle East at CUNY's Brooklyn College. Petersen-Overton was terminated after Dov Hikind, a pro-Israel member of the New York State Assembly, wrote to Brooklyn College to complain that Petersen-Overton's syllabus was overly critical of Israel and promoted suicide bombings. Petersen-Overton was reinstated after protest by hundreds of academics at CUNY and elsewhere.

Steven Salaita, professor of English at Virginia Polytechnic Institute and State University. In 2013, the University of Illinois at Urbana-Champaign offered Salaita a tenured faculty position, only for the university's chancellor to withdraw the offer the next year. The chancellor cited intemperate comments Salaita made on Twitter during the 2014 bombardment of Gaza. Salaita became a cause célèbre and won an $875,000 settlement against the university, yet was unable to find academic work in the United States. After taking a one-year position at the American University of Beirut (AUB), a search committee there recommended he be offered a permanent position, at which point AUB's president cancelled the search. Salaita's supporters expressed concern that "AUB is reproducing the trend of persecuting scholars who condemn the injustices in Palestine." Salaita now drives a school bus outside Washington DC.

Rabab Abdulhadi, ethnic studies professor at San Francisco State University. In 2014, Abdulhadi made a presentation about a recent trip to the Middle East in which she offered what she later described as "criticism of Israel state policy and Palestinian conditions under occupation." The AMCHA Initiative, which describes its mandate as opposing campus anti-Semitism, accused Abdulhadi of misrepresenting her trip, which it alleged had included meetings with more than one "known terrorist." AMCHA, whose allegations were cosigned by seven other organizations, charged that Abdulhadi's presentation contributed to a "hostile environment" for Jewish students. After an investigation, the university found the allegations to be without merit. Despite this finding, the university subsequently audited Abdulhadi's international travel from the preceding five years.

Abdulhadi continues to be embroiled in controversy, which she has sometimes exacerbated with defiant rhetoric expressing intolerance for opposing views (e.g., "Zionists are NOT welcomed on our campus"). Abdulhadi, in turn, has been denounced as a "collaborator with terrorists" and a promoter of "Jewhatred" in posters put up around her campus by the David Horowitz Freedom Center, a conservative think tank that some have accused of Islamophobia. In 2017, Abdulhadi also became the subject of a lawsuit initiated by the Lawfare Project, a New York organization that called itself "the legal arm of the pro-Israel community." The lawsuit was dismissed, but Abdulhadi is currently embroiled in a separate lawsuit against her university, which she alleges has discriminated against her.

In the years since the publication of "The Palestine Exception," pro-Palestinian students and scholars have continued to face challenges to their intellectual freedom. These include Paul Hedweh, a student at the University of California, Berkeley, who taught in a school program that allows undergraduates to teach a one-credit class. In 2016, Hedweh's class, Palestine: A Settler Colonial Analysis, was cancelled after the AMCHA Initiative sent a letter co-signed by forty-three organizations to Berkeley's chancellor protesting that the course was "intended to indoctrinate students to hate the Jewish state." The class was re-instated after a widespread public outcry.

Palestine Legal's most recent annual report indicates that in 2018 it responded to 289 incidents of suppression, noting that of these, "76 percent targeted students and scholars at 68 campuses across the country." There may be no other group in American academia whose intellectual freedom is so precarious. In this way, the Palestinian exception reveals the shortcomings of two dogmatic narratives about campus speech.

The first is a narrative of conservative martyrdom. It frames academia as singularly intolerant of right-of-centre views. "In case after case, I've seen conservative professors fired or punished in spite of possessing superior academic credentials," David French wrote in a representative article in *National Review* in 2017, which mentioned no cases involving non-conservatives. Violations of the intellectual freedom of conservative professors and speakers are a serious problem, but constant repetition of the conservative narrative has given rise to the false belief that they have no equivalent elsewhere on the political spectrum.

The second dogma is one of liberal complacency. Although this narrative comes from the left, it is reactionary in the literal sense that it approaches the campus speech debate with the sole goal of rebutting conservative complaints.

A 2018 article by Chris Ladd in *Forbes* is typical. "Our phoney free speech crisis is a pet theory of people triggered to sputtering outrage by a black man who fails to stand for the national anthem," Ladd writes, referring to former National Football League quarterback Colin Kaepernick. "Whining like pampered little snowflakes, they scramble to establish some form of 'safe space.'" Like other proponents of this view, Ladd is so concerned with turning conservative hyperbole back on itself that he ends up advocating free-speech quietism. Hence his article's headline, "There Is No Free Speech Crisis on Campus," which sums up a view also frequently heard on progressive social media.

The Palestinian exception is a free-speech crisis on campus. It should be recognized as such, even if one has doubts about the Boycott, Divestment and Sanctions campaign. Plausible critics of that campaign include Noam Chomsky, whose credentials as an outspoken critic of Israel are impeccable.

Chomsky has argued that the BDS campaign is fatally limited by having as one of its goals a mass return of Palestinian refugees to Israel, as "there is virtually no meaningful support for [mass return] beyond the BDS movement itself." BDS may well be an unrealistic movement, yet one that some may argue still deserves reluctant and partial support, because it is one of the few forces pressuring Israel to improve its treatment of Palestinians.

But even if one were to concede that BDS is totally misguided, the assault on the academic freedom of its advocates should still be seen as unacceptable. At issue is whether pro-Palestinian advocates can engage in free inquiry, not whether they are beyond criticism.

There have been cases of BDS proponents seeking to suppress the speech of others. They include an incident at the University of California, Irvine, in which SJP disrupted a presentation by Reservists of Duty, an anti-BDS group made up of Israel Defense Forces veterans. Video of the 2018 event shows protestors chanting to drown out the reservists, who calmly respond by holding up an Israeli flag and a sign saying, "Do you want to talk or do you want to shout?" Similarly, even though Salaita regularly distinguished Zionism from Judaism, there is no possible defence of his tweet about the 2014 Gaza War that said, "by eagerly conflating Jewishness and Israel, Zionists are partly responsible when people say antisemitic shit in response to Israeli terror."

The problem with opponents of BDS and pro-Palestinian voices is that they go far beyond criticism, and seek systematic suppression. The case of Abu El-Haj, the Barnard anthropologist, is instructive. The language she employed in her aforementioned 2001 book, *Facts on the Ground: Archaeological Practice and Territorial Self-Fashioning in Israeli Society* (which predated BDS), was sober and restrained. Yet despite the scholarly care she took in expressing her views, she was still vilified in a manner meant to remove her from her job.

In the years since Abu El-Haj's case, pro-Israel entities have devoted extraordinary energy and resources to suppressing speech supportive of BDS, regardless of what form it takes. In 2015, for example, US casino magnate Sheldon Adelson and media proprietor Haim Saban convened a conference said to have raised "at least $20 million" to push back against BDS campus activism. Similarly, Israeli prime minister Benjamin Netanyahu is reported to have met with senior cabinet ministers to strategize against BDS. According to the *Jerusalem Post*, one proposal raised at the meeting was to encourage "anti-boycott legislation in friendly capitals around the world, such as Washington, Ottawa and Canberra."

US politicians needed little prodding. Since 2014, twenty-seven US states have introduced anti-BDS legislation. In February 2019, the US Senate passed "The Combating BDS Act of 2019," which states that anti-BDS laws at the state level cannot be pre-empted by federal law. The future of that legislation in the House of Representatives is uncertain. (In July, the House passed a non-binding resolution condemning BDS, but the Senate bill, which is more consequential, may generate more resistance.) Regardless of whether or not Washington ultimately passes binding anti-BDS legislation, the extraordinary interest that senators and Members of Congress have taken in condemning BDS sends a speech-chilling message of its own, and only encourages further censorship at the local level.

In addition to trying to censor BDS out of existence through legislation, critics of BDS also have made use of civil-rights lawsuits. Title VI of the Civil Rights Act prohibits discrimination by institutions that receive federal funding. The AMCHA Initiative, the Zionist Organization of America and other non-government organizations sympathetic to Israel have filed half a dozen Title VI complaints targeting pro-Palestinian activities at public universities, arguing that they serve to create a hostile environment for Jewish students. To date, every complaint has been rejected. But even when they are denied, lawsuits still have the potential to chill speech. This has been pointed out by Kenneth Marcus, former general counsel for the Louis D. Brandeis Center for Human Rights Under Law, who helped formulate this legal strategy:

> Seeing all these cases rejected has been frustrating and disappointing, but we are, in fact, comforted by knowing that we are having the effect we had set out to achieve . . . These cases—even when rejected—expose administrators to bad publicity . . . No university wants to be accused of creating an abusive environment . . . Israel haters now publicly complain that these cases make it harder for them to recruit new adherents . . . Needless to say, getting caught up in a civil rights complaint is not a good way to build a resume or impress a future employer.

Future complaints may be more successful: Marcus is now the assistant secretary of education for civil rights at the US Department of Education, where Title VI cases are decided.

The AMCHA Initiative, the Brandeis Center, and similar groups view themselves as countering anti-Semitism. The definition of anti-Semitism they employ, however, has long been controversial. According to the so-called State Department definition, anti-Semitic expression includes not only prejudicial expression about Jews but also the "Three D's": demonizing Israel, delegitimizing Israel, and holding Israel to a double standard. The expanded definition is a response to a genuine problem, that of anti-Semitic speech cloaked as criticism of Israel. The State Department definition however, particularly as it is wielded by pro-Israel NGOs, goes too far the other way, and labels fair criticisms of Israel as racist. AMCHA co-founder Tammi Rossman-Benjamin, for example, has said that under the State Department definition, all BDS activity would qualify as anti-Semitic (as would mock eviction notices).

Beyond civil rights lawsuits and a weaponized definition of anti-Semitism, pro-Palestinian scholars and activists have also had to contend with a more basic obstacle: the increasingly pervasive ideology of intellectual "safety," which encourages students to view disagreeable political speech as psychologically harmful. Writers of letters and emails sent to the University of Illinois chancellor during the Salaita controversy applied this tactic. One message read, "as a Jewish student I would NOT feel safe in his classroom." Another asked: "Do you want to run a university where your students don't feel safe?" Similarly, when SJP launched a campaign to encourage DePaul University to divest from companies involved in Israel's occupation of Palestinian territory, *Breitbart*'s coverage was headlined, "Jewish DePaul student: 'I no longer felt safe on campus.'"

Of course, the ideology of safety is not a result of pro-Israel NGOs coaching students. It is a habit of mind that increasingly comes naturally to well-intentioned people, who overlook the threat to open inquiry and debate that can result from viewing deep political disagreements, a normal feature of campus life, as a threat. The same danger holds for appeals to "civility," which were deployed in regard to the removal of Finkelstein and Salaita, and for claims that criticisms of Israel create a "hostile environment" for Jewish students. These familiar tropes portray students as intellectually fragile creatures who need to be protected from dangerous ideas. The ease with which they can lead to curtailing free inquiry has of course been documented many times, most often by critics of "political correctness." But the Palestinian exception shows that progressive causes can themselves be silenced in the name of sensitivity.

In recent decades, the right to free inquiry has lost some of its progressive sheen. This was observed by Ronald Dworkin in the 1990s, when he gloomily noted how the images and associations conjured by "academic freedom" had changed over his lifetime. For leftists of Dworkin's generation, who came of age in the 1960s, academic freedom brought to mind communist professors and opposition to loyalty oaths. "Liberals and radicals were all for academic freedom. Many conservatives thought it overrated or even part of the conspiracy to paint America red," Dworkin wrote in *Freedom's Law* (1996). By the 1990s, however, the idea of academic freedom more often was applied to battle campus speech codes prohibiting allegedly racist and sexist utterances. "Now it is the party of reform that talks down academic freedom and conservatives who call it a bulwark of western civilization," Dworkin observed ruefully. His response to this development was to reaffirm academic freedom as a deeply egalitarian value.

The right to free inquiry has often been defended on instrumental grounds. According to that defence, a society that upholds academic freedom is more likely to discover important intellectual truths. But there are possible restrictions on academic freedom, such as a narrow ban on universities hiring Holocaust deniers or 9/11 truthers, that would seem to present no barrier to uncovering the truth. So while advancing the truth is one part of the rationale for academic freedom, purely instrumental defences are not enough.

As noted earlier in this essay, we also need academic freedom because of the role it plays in exemplifying what Dworkin called "ethical individualism." This is the value liberal societies uphold in protecting individual conviction and its expression. It is based on the idea that each of us has the right, and the responsibility, to determine for ourselves what gives shape to a valuable life. Fulfilling this responsibility requires the freedom to live and speak in accord with the truth as we see it.

This responsibility, of devoting ourselves to the truth, is incorporated in different occupations to different degrees. Salespeople, for example, cannot lie, but they are also not obliged to give a strictly neutral description of their products. Doctors are held to a higher standard than telemarketers, but even their strong commitment to the truth can be qualified by concern with what is in the best interests of a patient to hear. Of all vocations, academics have the greatest obligation to pursue the truth. Their occupation entails, in Dworkin's words, "an undiluted responsibility to the truth, and it is, in that way, the closest a professional responsibility can come to the fundamental ethical responsibility each of us has, according to the ideals of ethical individualism, to live his life in accordance with his own felt convictions."

The ethical defence, in short, values academic freedom not just because it helps us discover the truth. Academic freedom also provides a model of what it is to live in truth, which is ultimately the concern of everyone. So even though members of Students for Justice in Palestine are not academic researchers, in devoting themselves to a political cause they, too, are exercising ethical individualism, as are student groups with opposing views on Israel-Palestine.

Contempt for ethical individualism is at the root of why authoritarian regimes in Hungary, Turkey, and elsewhere are so hostile to academic freedom. Such freedom contributes to a culture of independence in the wider society. In this way, robust academic freedom is a mortal threat to the culture of conformity that takes purest form under authoritarianism, but which can also occur in democracies, as during the McCarthy period. As Dworkin warned, "an invasion of academic freedom is ... dangerous for everyone because it weakens the culture of independence and cheapens the ideal that culture protects."

What expression is protected by academic freedom, and what is allowed under the law, are separate questions. For its part, the ethical conception of academic freedom does not protect every imaginable form of expression. Burning a cross on the lawn of a historically black college; spray-painting a Swastika in a Jewish student's dorm; using (as opposed to merely mentioning) racial slurs: None of these forms of expression is protected by academic freedom, because each is clearly motived by a conscious intent to cause distress. No one's ability to live in truth is compromised by being asked to communicate in a manner that avoids deliberate cruelty.

This limit to academic freedom is worth emphasizing because it is at odds with the far more restrictive conception of academic inquiry that proponents of the Palestinian exception, however unwittingly, enforce. This is evident in many methods they employ. But the ideology of safety, which increasingly informs the use of all other tools, including anti-BDS legislation, may provide the clearest example.

Whether a statement is a threat to someone's "safety" is now widely seen as a matter of its impact on the hearer. According to the ethical conception of academic freedom, however, hurt feelings are not grounds to restrict speech and inquiry. This is not because the impact of our words is a trivial matter, or because college students today are sensitive little snowflakes. Academic freedom applies to a relationship, that between hearer and speaker, and in determining if someone has gone beyond the proper bounds of free inquiry, we need to give some weight to the interests of the speaker. In particular, we need to consider what motivated the speech in question. Only in cases in which causing distress is not a mere side effect of trying to get at the truth, but a speaker's deliberate goal, does academic freedom fail to apply. We apply a counter-factual test: Would the person have said what they said if they did not think it would hurt the listener? By that standard, cross-burnings, swastikas, and racial slurs fail. Speech that is incidentally distressing—including controversial political advocacy—does not.

There are many ways in which participating in academic life can cause us to feel indignant, startled, or even wounded. A historian might demonstrate that some beloved leader or ancestor was a monster; a philosophy professor might challenge our most cherished religious beliefs; a theologian or a women's studies professor might call into question our views on abortion or sex. Viewing the offence that free inquiry can cause as grounds to restrict it is incompatible with the proper working of academia, a major function of which is to give life to a culture of independence. Making that culture available to everyone will always permit no exceptions, Palestinian or otherwise.

SYNCOPES

Wayne Grady

One morning, after a minor abdominal operation (inguinal hernia, apparently everyone gets them), I lay in my hospital bed for four hours, as instructed, then sat on the side of the bed for twenty more minutes, also as instructed, before attempting to stand up. I didn't want to go to the patients' lounge, particularly; I just wanted to see how much it hurt to walk. There is something about pain that makes us want to explore it, or test ourselves against it: the tongue in the abscessed tooth, the relationship we know is wrong.

As soon as I got to the lounge, the room began to spin; the glass doors to the patio grew wobbly and opaque; the shrubbery behind them blurred, and a loud roar filled my ears. I sank onto a chair, my forehead clammy with sweat, and sat for several minutes holding the table in front of me, working hard at not falling off the chair. The nurses had warned us about this. We were not to fall: we might break something, a lamp or a hip. I was in the Shouldice Hospital, in Toronto; all they do is hernias. A few days earlier, a patient had fallen and broken a rib and had had to be taken to Sunnybrook Hospital for treatment. The nurses were still talking about it. As I sat in the chair waiting for the upheaval to subside, I wasn't thinking about falling or not falling; I was simply trembling and sweating and waiting, like a mouse cornered by a cat. All right, you've got me—now get it over with. After a long time, maybe five minutes, the patio doors stopped warping and, still dazed but coming out of it, I stumbled the remaining distance to the nursing station, where I was barely able to gasp: "I need help."

One of the duty nurses looked up, rushed around the counter, and grabbed my arm. She and another nurse led me back to the patients' lounge and told me to lie down on a couch. Bending down to a couch with a fresh groin wound, no matter how expertly sutured, is not an enjoyable experience. If I were a medieval knight, I would be easing myself to the ground, resolved to die. I am not a medieval knight. The second nurse brought a blood-pressure gauge.

"A hundred and seventeen over sixty-two," she said, frowning.

"That's too low," the first nurse said. "You should have called us. You might have fallen and broken something."

"I know, I'm sorry."

"Next time," she said, "call us as soon as you start to feel dizzy. Just call out, we'll hear you. Or lie down on the floor where someone can see you." I pictured myself sitting on the hospital floor in my johnny shirt, asking a fellow patient to call a nurse. No, I would not have done that.

"I will," I said. "I'm sorry."

Satisfied, the second nurse took me back to my room in a wheelchair and helped me onto the bed. Even that felt demeaning. I thanked her. When she left, I lay on the bed looking up at the ceiling, wondering why my default emotional settings always seemed to be guilt, shame, and gratitude.

In Vladimir Nabokov's memoir, *Speak, Memory*, he recalls the moment, shortly after the 1917 revolution, when he and his family emigrated from Russia. "The break in my own destiny," he writes, "affords me in retrospect a syncopal kick that I would not have missed for worlds."

Nabokov had what many writers have who write in a language that is not their first: a finicky delight in finding the exact but somewhat arcane word. In this passage, the eye snags on "syncopal." Masha Gessen mentions this word in her essay, "To Be, or Not to Be," in an issue of the *New York Review of Books* I had on the nightstand in my room in the Shouldice. I read it in those pain-filled hours following my surgery, and it helped. She writes about her own emigration from the Soviet Union to the United States, quoting Nabokov and noting that the word "syncope" has a rich variety of meanings. "In linguistics," she says, "it's the shortening of a word by omission of a sound or syllable from its middle; in music, it is a change of rhythm and shift of accent when a normally weak beat is stressed. . ." In other words, a syncope can be either a significant absence or an accentuated presence. "In medicine," she adds, "it is a brief loss of consciousness."

Syncope, then, refers to a thing that was there, has been forgotten, and then suddenly is there again. Like consciousness. While absent from memory, the thing continues to exist in the abstract, or theoretical, realm, but is no longer tangible in the here and now. Proust's forgotten and then vividly recalled madeleine was a syncopal kick that launched a thousand memories of his childhood. As a boy, Nabokov stood in a line-up waiting to be allowed to leave his homeland, and subsequently forgot that no doubt emotionally painful event. Then suddenly, perhaps through the very act of writing, the experience came rushing back into his conscious memory; hence, syncopal. If the two walls of the Grand Canyon were to close up, say by some cataclysmic seismic event, so that one could step from the South Rim to the North Rim without being aware of even a crack in the ground, the Grand Canyon would be a syncope. But only if it were recalled when a sign or monument was placed on the spot, "Here lay the former

Grand Canyon." To satisfy the medical criterion, it has to be temporarily lost to consciousness, and so in need of a monument or hotel to jog the memory and provide a mysterious but instantly explicable reason for its having been in that particular place.

For Nabokov, the cataclysmic events of 1917 had closed forever his beloved Russia. *Speak, Memory* was his monument to it—the first two hundred and fifty pages are taken up with detailed memories of czarist Russia that came back to him in a Proustian flood as he wrote. He had put the actual moment of emigration out of his mind, hadn't thought of it in years, and then there it was, lit up like a grand hotel in the middle of the desert.

In her essay, Gessen also refers to Suketu Mehta, a journalist who emigrated from India to the United States and who wrote, in his memoir *Maximum City: Bombay Lost and Found* (2005), that "Each person's life is dominated by a central event, which shapes and distorts everything that comes after it and, in retrospect, everything that comes before." The cataclysmic event doesn't have to be emigration. For many of my father's generation, it was the Second World War, which divided everything that went before it from everything that came after, and about which afterwards many would not speak. Or more specifically, some traumatizing incident connected with the war was subsequently withdrawn from their memories: dropping a bomb on a hospital or school, for example, or shooting a prisoner. They would talk hesitantly about the war, carefully skirting any mention of hospitals or prisoners. They talked about what could be had for a pair of silk stockings or a square of chocolate. Much contemporary German literature is written by the grandchildren of Second World War veterans; these writers, after a generation of silence, have begun to exantlate what their grandparents' generation had been incapable of mentioning. My father witnessed the sinking of a German U-boat in the North Atlantic; when he finally talked about it, he said that his ship had picked up the survivors. But, as historians often say about wars, things happen. He didn't say all the survivors. It was also during the war that my father passed for white— he left Windsor a single black man, and came back a married white man—for him, the war was the cataclysmic event that closed the chasm between his life before and his life after. In a sense, he did emigrate: by passing, he left the country of being black to dwell in the country of being white. The moment of passing was, for him, a syncope, about which he would not speak, would in fact forget. Was it the moment he was recruited into the navy, which was not accepting blacks at the that time? Did he ever stop waiting for the error to be discovered and corrected? Passing was both a lacuna and a hugely significant marker, his closed and forgotten Grand Canyon—to which, by writing my novel *Emancipation Day*, I put up a monument.

"What happened to me back there?" I asked the nurse who was walking me up and down the hall. Not exactly holding my arm, but ready to. I was in "some discomfort," as nurses call excruciating pain. We passed a dozen similarly stricken patients, most of them men in their seventies wearing flannel pyjamas and slippers, also two younger women in track suits, and one fourteen-year-old boy who'd been born with a herniated navel and had finally had it repaired. I nodded slightly as I passed them, and they nodded slightly back. Even nodding caused us some discomfort.

"I almost fainted," I said to the nurse.

"It's called syncope," she replied, pronouncing the word with three syllables: sin-*co*-pee. In English, the terminal "e" is usually silent, as in scope, but this time it's accentuated, and so the word "syncope" is itself a syncope. Pronouncing foreign words in English is often an exercise in syncopation.

"What caused it?"

"Standing too abruptly after sitting or lying down," she said. "That causes a sudden lowering of blood pressure, and if your blood pressure is already low, as it often is after an operation, the result is a temporary loss of consciousness. You faint."

I hadn't fainted, but I had been in a kind of dream-like state between consciousness and loss of consciousness, as if I'd been dreaming about standing under a waterfall. I imagined blood draining from my brain and pooling in my heart, and my heart being too weak to pump it back up again. This may be literally inaccurate, an example of what Merilyn, my wife, refers to as "Grady's Anatomy." But it seemed to me to be metaphorically true. A strong shock to the nerves can also cause a lowering of blood pressure; we turn pale as the blood rushes from the brain, and whether it swells the heart or not, the heart is thought of as the seat of the emotions, the vessel into which blood drains from the brain. In Victorian literature, characters experiencing sudden rushes of emotion—declarations of love, news of the death of a loved one, financial disasters—collapse onto various divans, chaises longues or "fainting couches" placed there for the purpose, and have their wrists patted or are given smelling salts or brandy. They swoon. Mystery novelists emphasize the importance of preparing a person to receive bad news, and detectives tend to regard the absence of swooning as an indication of prior knowledge, if not of actual guilt.

The heart swells—with love, or pride, or courage. But these emotions are experienced by the same organ that experiences thought: the brain. Feeling emotion drains blood from the brain; reasoning floods the brain with a rush of blood. Thus, both reason and passion are related to the sanguinal tide flowing to and from the brain. We feel not with our hearts but with our brains: *Sentio ergo sum*. I feel, therefore I am.

When I was thirteen, faithfully every Sunday morning in church I fainted. I was in the choir, so my swoons were visible to all. Whenever we rose to sing after a lengthy prayer or sermon, I would feel an unpleasant light-headedness, a terrifying roar would fill my ears, and the next thing I knew I'd be lying on a bench in the vestry with the minister, a portly, white-haired gentleman, fanning me with a hymnal while my father, the choirmaster, looked on with a mixture of concern and embarrassment. If we had lived in rural Quebec, my swooning might have been a cause for rejoicing, taken for a deeply religious experience, an influx of the Holy Spirit, and I might have been whisked off to a seminary to become a priest. But we were in Protestant Ontario, a land of practical, no-nonsense Orangemen and Odd Fellows, and my fainting was seen merely as a temporary interruption in the weekly business of getting on with church and back to the barn. I'd be given a glass of water and left to recover on my own, while Reverend Cathcart returned to the pulpit to finish the service.

I lay by myself in the vestry while the service went on next door. After a while I would get up, take off my surplice, and go outside to walk among the gravestones in the cemetery until the service was over. I felt like Mercy, in *Pilgrim's Progress,* abandoned outside the Celestial City while her mistress, Christiana, was being celebrated within. The Keeper of the Gate "opened the gate and looked out, but Mercy was fallen down without in a swoon, for she fainted and was afraid that no gate would be opened to her."

What I was really feeling was humiliation and a vague sense of guilt at having been the cause of such fuss, and regret that the fuss was still being made. When my fainting spells continued, off and on, for almost a year, Reverend Cathcart quietly suggested to my father that it might be better for all concerned if I left the choir and sat with my mother and brother in the congregation. My fainting spells stopped and were never mentioned again. Until that syncopal moment in the hospital, I had forgotten all about them.

When, forty years later, my father died of congestive heart failure, it was explained to me by his doctor that his heart had become too weak to pump fluid out of his lungs. "Think of the heart as a football," the doctor said. "When it loses muscle tone, it's like a football that deflates, it becomes shapeless, getting weaker and weaker until eventually it just quits." I came away from this with a vague sense that my father had drowned; his heart was less like a deflated football than like a failed bilge pump whose warranty had run out. (This might be another excerpt from *Grady's Anatomy*, but I like the bilge-pump analogy because of its nautical association. Most examples of syncopated words I can think of have a tang of the sea about them: foc's'le, bosun, gunnel, stun's'l. It's as though sailors are too busy to pronounce the middles of words.)

In "Can a Bombay Strongman Explain Trump?"—an op-ed piece in the *New York Times* that appeared in January 2017—Suketu Mehta compares Trump's rise to the US presidency with the similarly alarming accession to power in India by Bal Keshav Thackeray, a Bombay crime boss who founded the Shiv Sena Party in 1966, and who, by means of thuggery, corruption, and intimidation, ruled the city of Bombay in the turbulent 1990s. Like Trump, "Thackeray . . . rode to power on a wave of outrageous stories, bluster, lies, bigotry and showmanship," writes Mehta. Thackeray referred to his opponents as "vampires" and "a sack of flour," approved of Adolf Hitler, and regularly called for books and films to be banned if he disagreed with their authors or producers. "Egged on by his invective," says Mehta, "his legions would go out and beat up artists and journalists."

A man named Sunil, one of Thackeray's lieutenants, told Mehta that what Thackeray's army had was "powertoni." Sunil hired a Muslim boy in the Muslim locality for his cable business, Mehta writes in *Maximum City*. Sunil told him that the boy "has twelve brothers and six sisters. I gave him money and his brother liquor. He will even beat up his brother for me. I hire him for powertoni." It took Mehta a while to realize that "powertoni" was a contraction of "power of attorney"—in other words, a syncope—but it meant much more than simply having the authority to make legal decisions for someone else. Powertoni is "the awesome ability to act on someone else's behalf or to have others do your bidding, to sign documents, release wanted criminals, cure illnesses, get people killed." When Thackeray assumed power, he changed the name Bombay to Mumbai, and no one in the city dared refer to it by its anglicized name. As a person with powertoni, Thackeray claimed he was giving voice to people who had had none of their own—the millions of Hindu workers in Mumbai who had been marginalized when the city switched from an industrial economy to a financial and service centre when low-paying, blue-collar jobs disappeared and were replaced by positions for people with degrees and suits. Thackeray promised to "turn back the clock"; in other words, he would drain the swamp, he would make Mumbai great again.

"We watched all the big people—ministers, business-men—bow and touch his feet," said a friend of Sunil's. Even though Thackeray's followers had, in reality, relinquished any power they had to a tyrant. "Every time one of the corporate gods or a member of the city's film community or a politician from Delhi kowtowed before him, his boys got a thrill of pride, and their image of the Saheb as a powerful man, a man with powertoni, was reinforced." Even as their own power vanished.

After breakfast, I went back to my room to read, but couldn't manage more than a page without falling asleep. It seemed the painkillers also killed consciousness. I dreamed I was on a crowded bus, or perhaps in a covered boat, and a woman seated in front of me asked: "Do you feel better now, after your suicide attempt?" I woke in a panic, and there was the nurse, holding out a paper cup with two codeine tablets.

"After this," she said, "no more codeine. Only ibuprofen."

The pain in my abdomen still lurked in the severed muscle, in the solid, sutured ridge that ran under my skin like a length of rebar, and declared itself with every sudden movement. It hurt to laugh. It hurt to cough. We regarded new arrivals with a kind of smug suspicion, knowing what they were in for, and wondered if any of them had colds or the flu. It hurt even more to sneeze.

The Latin word for "mercy" is *misericordia*, which derives from *misericors*, which in turn derives from *cor*, the heart. Mercy, then, is a kind of misery of the heart. We also get the word "miser" from *miseria*, on the theory that a person who hoards money must be perpetually unhappy, or disheartened. But *miser* can also mean "erotic love," which brings us back to the swollen heart. What does lonely Roy Orbison say when he sees a pretty woman: "Mercy!"

Two days after the surgery, I signed up for a therapeutic massage. I was expecting a pleasant pummelling of my back and shoulders. Instead, my forty-minute session, given by a young Russian emigrée who talked the entire time, consisted of a light brushing of her fingertips over my chest and abdomen in clockwise rotation, as though she were finger-painting circles on my skin. "To stimulate lymph nodes," she explained, "to reroute the lymphatic circulation from your clavicles and axillaries." She fluttered her fingers over my collarbone and armpits. "And down to the nodes in your groin, so the lymphatic flow, which was interrupted by your incision, will go around it, from left side to right, and continue down to your legs."

"My legs?" I said.

"The calves," she said. "The calf is what we call 'the second heart.' You have heard this?"

"No," I said. "A second heart?"

"Two second hearts," she said. "One in each calf."

"What do they do?"

"They pump the lymphatic material back up into your body. Every time you take a step you activate these little hearts."

Her husband, also Russian, was a master of Qigong, a Chinese discipline that is both a psychic exercise and a martial art, a kind of militarized tai chi. "Good for lowering high blood pressure," she said. I once witnessed a Qigong session in China, in a remote village in the northern Gobi Desert, and was not inclined to scoff. "He moves his hands over my body, much as I am doing for you, very lightly and without touching." I nodded. The woman in the school gymnasium in China had fluttered her hands over people's backs and down the sides of their legs, caused grown men and women to strut and crow like roosters, and others to collapse in a dead faint on the cement floor. "In this way he moves the energy around," my therapist said, "and rids the body of impurities, giving it much power." And giving the Qigong master powertoni. "Then he touches my body, oh, just the smallest, lightest touch, but oh my God."

When I returned to my room, I looked up "lymph nodes" on Wikipedia. There were drawings of typical nodes; kidney-shaped capsules perched atop stems, or lymph vessels, like beans thrust up from the ground on their own roots. A node was described as consisting of two sections, an outer cortex wrapped around a central medulla—both terms usually associated with the brain. In the drawing, the node was brain-shaped. A tiny organ that pumps like a heart and looks like a brain.

I thought about my dream. I don't usually think about dreams, or very much enjoy other people telling me about theirs, but this one evoked a clear memory that I had thought was a happy one.

When Merilyn and I were in Scotland, in 1999, we took a tour boat from Anstruther, in Fyfe, to the Isle of May, five miles out into the Firth of Forth, to see a colony of Sandwich terns that populated the island. The water was rough and it was a small boat, built for the in-shore herring fishery, and there were perhaps twenty of us on board, standing and sitting in a tight, enclosed cabin to keep out of the rain. Halfway to the island, the boat's propellers became entangled in a fisherman's net; the engine stalled, and we spent three hours bobbing and rolling in the Firth while someone with a knife tried to cut the propellers free.

Everyone was sick. There was a bathroom that no one wanted to go near, and numerous dashes to the rail. I stood at the centre of the cabin, holding onto a cage above my head that housed the life jackets. I don't usually get seasick, but this time I could feel nausea creeping over me: the cold sweat, the roaring, the dizziness as I tried to fix my eyes on something, anything, that wasn't moving. Through one of the portholes I saw the cliffs of the Isle of May rising and falling, and though I felt the blood draining from my face and my eyes glazing over, the air in the cabin growing warmer and reeking of vomit, I did not throw up or faint. Finally, the crew cleared the propellers and the boat began to make way. Merilyn hadn't been sick, either. She'd sat on one of the benches against the bulkhead, pale and drawn but a picture of grim determination. When the boat docked, she came over to me.

"Are you feeling better now?" she asked.

It was a pleasant memory. I was feeling better. We saw the terns; we walked through the famous lighthouse built by Robert Louis Stevenson's grandfather. I've often thought about the Isle of May and the birds, but had forgotten about the crossing, just as Nabokov had thought fondly about England, his years at Cambridge, his decision to write in English, and had forgotten the terrifying moment of exile from his beloved Russia.

But where did that question of suicide come from? I could only think it had something to do with the hernia operation, with being voluntarily cut open—a failed attempt, because I was sewn back up again—and the ensuing pain. If emotions come from the brain, then dreams may be the expression of emotions, not thoughts, and should be considered as images of feelings we can't otherwise articulate: I was feeling as though I had survived a suicide attempt.

In order to prepare for the operation, I'd been told to lose ten pounds. I lost thirty, and when I left the Shouldice I had to buy new clothes. I went into a leather shop and looked at belts, and the smell of new leather triggered another syncopal kick: I suddenly remembered visiting my father in another hospital when I was ten or eleven years old. It was deep winter. He'd slipped a disk while lifting a bag of coal from the trunk of our car. After his operation, he was laid up for three weeks in Sunnybrook Hospital, in Toronto. When my mother and brother and I visited him, we found him sitting up in bed, reading a book, the only book I ever saw him read in his entire life: a novel by Louis L'Amour with a cowboy on the cover.

I noticed it not only because it was the only time I had seen him reading, but also because I myself was writing a novel at the time. My hero was an American GI named Sergeant Rock, and all I remember about the book now is that, like the comic books from which I'd stolen the character, it was a relentlessly episodic account of Rock's heroic exploits, during the Second World War, taking hill after hill, knocking out machine-gun nest after machine-gun nest. Looking at the comic books now, I realize that each Sergeant Rock story had a moral to it, something poignant about loyalty or courage or manhood. There was none of that in my novel. The Sarge and his men took a hill, then moved to eliminate a machine-gun nest, then took another hill. That was war. I was also writing a long poem about Sir Francis Drake's voyage around the world, about which I knew even less than I did about the Second World War.

But I felt involved in literature, and seeing my father reading a book stirred up a complicated succession of emotions in me, surprise followed by reassessment and confirmation. Maybe I didn't have to conceal from him the fact that I was sitting up in my room at night with a flashlight, hiding my scribblers under the mattress during the day. Maybe I could talk to my father about something interesting, like Drake's sailing around the Horn in a force-9 gale. But even at that age I was dismissive of Louis L'Amour: in school, I was reading good books, *Robinson Crusoe* and *Pinocchio*, and memorizing poems by Rudyard Kipling. "If you can keep your head when all about you / Are losing theirs and blaming it on you." Kipling to me was the ideal father, passing on wise advice to his son, whereas I remember only one occasion when my father tried to give me some advice: the day before I left home to go to university, he took me aside and told me not to "go hopping into bed with the first woman who comes along and drops her drawers," which, although I cringed at the crudity of his remark, was exactly what I intended to do at the first opportunity. And so, Louis L'Amour notwithstanding, I didn't feel my father was someone in whom I could confide, or even reveal my nascent interest in becoming a writer.

When he looked up and saw us come into his room, he smiled and put down his book. I think he even apologized for reading it: "Someone left it in the room." We kissed him lightly on the cheek and my mother asked him how he was feeling. She gave him a pair of slippers she'd knitted, for when he was able to get up and walk around, and he gave my brother and me belts he had made from kits given to him as part of a recovery therapy program. The belts consisted of a series of black-and-white leather links woven together, a black, a white, a black, a white, with a black tongue at one end and a metal buckle at the other. The alternating black-and-white pattern had no significance for me at the time, as it would be another thirty years before I discovered he'd been hiding our African heritage from us, but I was touched that he had made something for me, and have loved the smell of new leather ever since.

A *misericorde* was a long, thin, stiletto-like knife used in the Middle Ages to put mortally wounded knights out of their misery. The blade was inserted through a small opening in the knight's armour, and driven in until it pierced the heart.

BEAUTY IS A METHOD

Christina Sharpe

> Beauty is not a luxury, rather it is a way of creating possibil-
> ity in the space of enclosure, a radical act of subsistence, an
> embrace of our terribleness, a transfiguration of the given.
> It is a will to adorn, a proclivity for the baroque, and the love
> of *too much.*
>
> — Saidiya Hartman, *Wayward Lives, Beautiful Experi-*
> *ments: Intimate Histories of Social Upheaval*

> Words set things in motion. I've seen them doing it. Words
> set up atmospheres, electrical fields, charges. I've felt them
> doing it. Words conjure. I try not to be careless about what I
> utter, write, sing. I'm careful about what I give voice to.
>
> — Toni Cade Bambara, "What It Is I think I'm Doing
> Anyhow."

vessel:

a container (such as a cask, bottle, kettle, cup, or bowl) for hold-
ing something
a person into whom some quality (such as grace) is infused
a watercraft bigger than a rowboat; especially: ship
a tube or canal (such as an artery) in which a body fluid is con-
tained and conveyed or circulated

a conducting tube in the xylem of a vascular plant formed by
  the fusion and loss of end walls of a series of cells
More than flesh, a body—your "beat and beating heart."*

I've been revisiting what beauty as a method might mean
or do: what it might break open, rupture, make possible and
impossible. How we might carry beauty's knowledge with us
and make new worlds.

　　With all of the work that my parents did to try to enter
and stay in the middle class, precarity and more than precarity remained. That precarity looked and felt like winters without heat because there was no money for oil; holes in ceilings,
walls, and floors from water damage that we could not afford
to repair; the fears and reality of electricity and other utilities
being cut for non-payment; fear of a lien being placed on the
house because there was no, or not enough, money to pay
property taxes. But through all that and more, my mother tried
to make a small path through the wake. She brought beauty
into that house in every way that she could; she worked at joy,
and she made livable moments, spaces, and places in the midst
of all that was unlivable there, in the town we lived in; in the
schools we attended; in the violence we saw and felt inside the
home while my father was living and outside it in the larger
white world before, during, and after his death. Though she
was not part of any organized Black movements, except in how
one's life and mind are organized by and positioned to appre-
hend the world through the optic of the door and antiblack-
ness , my mother was politically and socially astute. She was
attuned not only to our individual circumstances but also to
those circumstances as they were an indication of, and related
to, the larger antiblack world that structured all of our lives.**

---

* Toni Morrison, *Beloved* (New York: Plume, 1987).
** Christina Sharpe, *In The Wake: On Blackness and Being* (Durham: Duke
University Press, 2016).

We lived in a town that used and hated and feared its Black population. I grew up in Wayne, Pennsylvania, at a four-way intersection: rich white folks in three directions and a small Black neighbourhood in the other. One bright, sunny summer day when I was eight or nine or ten years old, police from at least two townships, but I think three, descended on and laid siege to my neighbourhood. Multiple police cars blocked our streets because a white woman reported that she saw a Black man driving a station wagon through the centre of Wayne with a shotgun visible in the back. The Black man was named Chicki Carter—and he was really a boy, seventeen or eighteen years old. He was a friend of my brother Stephen. The rifle was a rake—part of the set of tools Chicki used for the yardwork he was doing that summer in order to earn money. We gathered in our front yards, on the sidewalks, and in the road; we ran after the police cars; and we witnessed and insisted loudly that Chicki had done nothing wrong. That day, at least, while there *was* harm done, it was not *immediately* fatal harm.

Knowing that every day that I left the house many of the people whom I encountered did not think me precious and showed me so, my mother gave me space to be precious—as in vulnerable, as in cherished. It is through her that I first learned that beauty is a practice, that beauty is a method, and that a vessel is also "a person into whom some quality (such as grace) is infused." *Dark Symphony: Negro Literature in America* was my mother's book. My brother Stephen gave it to her. There is an inscription in it, as there is in every book we gave each other: *Happy Birthday, To Mommy, Love Stephen, 3/2/70.* In the pages of the book is a list on a worn slip of paper—the top of the list is faded from sun and disintegrating. The list is in my mother's fast cursive—the writing she used when she was making notes to and for herself. My mother's handwriting for the world was meticulous (as in the note to me in the first edition of *Beloved* that she gave me on my twenty-third birthday). In rebellion against the nuns at West Catholic Girls' who tried to control every aspect of her school life, my mother had created her own beautifully ornate script. This particular list is written on the back of a form that she recycled from her job in human resources at Sears, Roebuck and Co., a sheet of light blue paper that she tore into strips to use as bookmarks: a lifelong habit instilled in a child of the Depression—use everything, waste nothing. The list:

Before the Mayflower ($3.95)
Malcolm X: The Man and His Time ($5.95)
*The Negro Handbook ($8.95)
A Pictorial History of the Negro in America ($4.95)
What Manner of Man ($4.95)
This Child's Gonna Live ($4.95)
*Contemporary Art in Africa ($7.25)
Black Political Power in America ($6.95)
Black Power U.S.A ($5.95)
The White Problem: ($6.95)
Confrontation: Black and White ($6.95)
To Be Young Gifted and Black (Lorraine Hansberry) ($6.95)
Black in White America ($5.95)

The bookmark marks the beginning of "Esther" from Jean Toomer's Cane.

I was a vessel for all of my mother's ambitions for me—ambitions that found their own shapes.

My mother made me a purple gingham dress with purple and lilac and blue appliqué tulips. She tried, over many summers, to teach me how to sew: needlepoint, appliqué, cross-stitch, slip stitch. She failed. We failed together. She had a beautiful old pedal-operated Singer sewing machine, and when you opened the shallow drawers that ran along the top they were filled with brightly coloured and differently weighted needlepoint yarn. I used to love to look at them. I would arrange and disarrange them, stack her thimbles, disturb her order.

When she was dying, my mother still made Christmas ornaments by hand. It was a shock on re-encountering the red felt hearts with the straight pins holding them together, the black felt globe with its own arrangement of pins—the ordinary flat-headed pins, the round red and white and brown heads. My mother's symmetry: even the bent pins have a place. It was a shock to encounter them again—the way that beauty shocks. But more. What is beauty made of? Attentiveness whenever possible to a kind of aesthetic that escaped violence whenever possible—even if it is only the perfect arrangement of pins.

I continue to think about beauty and its knowledges.

I learned to see in my mother's house. I learned how not to see in my mother's house. How to limit my sight to the things that could be controlled. I learned to see in discrete angles, planes, plots. If the ceiling was falling down and you couldn't do anything about it, what you could do was grow and arrange peonies and tulips and zinnias; cut forsythia and mock orange to bring inside.

My mother gifted me a love of beauty, a love of words. She gave me every Black book that was published—and, in her practice, birthdays always included gifts for the body, gifts for the mind, and gifts for the soul. The mind and the soul came together in books: novels, poetry, short stories, history, art. One of those books was Toni Cade Bambara's *The Salt Eaters* in which Bambara, in the dedication, thanks *her* mother, "who in 1948, having come upon me daydreaming in the middle of the kitchen floor, mopped around me." In that dedication, I saw something that my mother would do; I saw something that she had done. My mother gave me space to dream. For whole days at a time, she left me with and to words, curled up in a living-room windowsill, uninterrupted in my reading and imagining other worlds.

Some books I read in that windowsill: *The Complete Poems of Paul Laurence Dunbar*; *The People Could Fly: American*

Black Folktales; Dark Symphony: Negro Literature in America; Jane Eyre; Bright April; The Life of Ida B Wells: The Woman Who Killed Judge Lynch; Roll of Thunder, Hear My Cry; Little Women; Song of Solomon; The Life and Times of Frederick Douglass.

That window was my loophole of retreat—two feet deep, three feet wide, four feet high—the small public/private place from which I began to imagine myself into another world. The house was an old farmhouse, built in 1804, and there were no right angles in it—everything was on a slope. The windowsill I sat in looked out onto the backyard. In summer that meant cherries and quince, crabapple, greengage plum, four peony bushes, a huge weeping willow that had been struck by lightning, and beyond that the road called Radnor Street Road. There was also a vegetable garden where we grew tomatoes, corn, collard and mustard greens, turnips, kale, carrots, several varieties of lettuce, cucumbers, eggplant, zucchini, sweet and hot peppers, and more. In winter you could see the house behind the fruit trees where Chico and Joey lived. Sometimes the house was cold, and then my mother's stacks of newspapers became fireplace logs. And though this was a sign that there was no money for oil, there was an art to making my mother's neat paper logs: roll the paper, tuck one edge in, roll a little more, tuck the other edge. That way they wouldn't come undone. That way we wouldn't come undone.

> Beauty is a method:
> reading in the windowsill
> running after the police
> a list on a slip of paper in a book
> the arrangement of pins in cloth
> the ability to make firewood out of newspaper

This attentiveness to a Black aesthetic made me: moved me from the windowsill to the world.

SELFISH INTIMACY

Alexandra Molotkow

My parents sold their home recently, a small, vinyl-sided house at the end of a cul-de-sac, next to an eerie, overgrown hill where I once watched a hawk disembowel a squirrel. They've lived there since I was sixteen. Visiting over the holidays, I found myself caught between clashing perceptual modes: I wanted just to be there, enjoying the mundanity of a place that would soon be mythological to me. I also wanted to tour it like a stranger and send away dispatches—to friends who would never see it, to myself, who could never go back, to no one in particular.

My mother has always been a beautiful decorator, as well as a very good thrifter, and the house is sprouting with objects she's been accumulating since I was a girl. I took pictures of the lacquerware, the silk textiles, the exquisitely potted plants assembled in front of the window like overachieving siblings. I took pictures of family photographs; homemade greeting cards; a portrait of my uncle in the 1980s, painted by a friend of his, that my mom had restored after a basement leak and presented to me for my birthday. I was swamped with memories, but I found myself appraising every item by a strangely dispassionate standard—not so much what it had meant to me, but what I could "do" with it. I was gleaning the place for visual anecdotes suited to the person I am now.

Some pictures I texted to friends. Others I posted to my Instagram, which is slapdash and homely, with about as many followers as it deserves—I use the app like I once used Facebook, as a way of being ambiently with people I like, or to set up a dopamine drip while I'm doing something I'd rather not. My friends, flung out over the continent, were posting their own holiday or non-holiday pictures, and as much as I love my parents I felt homesick, as one does, for my independence. I live in a new city now, and Instagram was the simplest way to reconcile two lives.

My mother noticed what I was up to and eyed me uneasily. "Why do you have to *document* everything?" she said, as I snapped away at some erotic ceramicware. I told her I didn't plan to show anyone, but the point was that I could.

My mom and I have very different conceptions of privacy. This has been a steady source of conflict in our relationship. She is extremely careful about what she shares of her personal life, and with whom, whereas I've been flippant in the past about broadcasting mine. For a long time I didn't see a need to be discreet about my sex life, living habits, or childhood, and while I'm not ashamed of the details, I'm sometimes ashamed of the character I revealed. I regret having trespassed my mother's boundaries when our personal lives overlapped (I cleared this column with her beforehand). And it makes me sad, sometimes, to think of how callously I've treated my life, the ways I traded down experiences for anecdotes.

The divide is partly generational, of course. Like many million others I've been exposing myself long enough, in a workaday fashion, that gauging a moment's shareability—whether it's interesting, to whom, and at what valence—has become a reflex, which feels both like a pathology and a necessary life skill. I value privacy, but for me it doesn't feel at odds with self-exposure. The two seem related—I'd sooner post a picture of my messy apartment than let a friend come by; when I feel ugly, I find a good angle and post a selfie. Shaping your own image is mitigating when you feel vulnerable, a way to send out a decoy in your place.

For my mother, privacy is not just a personal boundary or a practical concern but an instinct, and something like an ethos: She has a deep revulsion to the idea of something private circulating in public context. She dislikes having her picture taken and hates having it shared; it removes her right to represent herself. She feels uneasy when she encounters other people's old, anonymous family photographs at flea markets. The shots might be totally banal—a woman standing barefoot on a lawn, or a child crying at the beach—but their very banality is demeaning; they meant a lot to *someone*.

When she first explained this to me, I didn't get it. I remembered a performance I saw years ago by the Trachtenburg Family Slideshow Players, a mom, dad, and daughter who collected strangers' old snapshots and made up songs about them. As a teenager I thought this was a neat schtick, and a nice gesture, a way of honouring the humble people traced by old slides. Now I think of how I'd feel were the artifacts of my life used as fodder for someone's art project, and it makes me very angry.

More and more, I understand my mother's circumspection: most of the time, what feels monumental to you is a trifle to anyone else; describing it out loud, absorbing an outside response, can put you at odds with your own emotions. Posting pictures of a loved one is, on one hand, like placing them on a work desk; on the other, it seems obscene to consider the image's likability. Posting pictures of friends means using their image, in some way, to augment your own, inviting the sort of self-presentational calculus from which friendships are, ideally, an oasis.

Relationships are subject to their own, encrypted terms; to air them publicly is to submit them for outside judgment, and risk letting something delicate and conditional wilt in the light. I often think of a clip featured in *Montage of Heck*, the 2015 Kurt Cobain documentary, in which Cobain is covertly filming himself kissing Courtney Love in bed. The closeup makes his face look fetal; you can hear the sucking sounds as their lips mash together, and her offhanded, guttural moans. Of all the home movies excerpted in the film, it gives the strongest impression of their chemistry, and it's absolutely disgusting.

Familial intimacy can have the same effect: I remember my discomfort when, as a child, I heard an adult I loved call his father "daddy," or when, in my twenties, I watched a boyfriend's mother scoop mushy leftovers of his favourite dish into a yogurt container. A certain idiosyncrasy might be vital to a relationship, and hold as much appeal out of context as a healthy organ removed from the body. There are few things more alienating, or revolting, or fascinating than other people's intimacy; it is literally *not for you*. There are few states more helpless than being exposed in your own.

As I circled my parents' house with my phone, I claimed to be acting in good faith. I wasn't posting Mom's image, or even taking her picture, just capturing what I loved about the home she'd made. But I knew I was acting obnoxiously. I was trailing the threat of an unknown audience through her space. She once told me, after a break-in, that above all else she'd felt vulnerable that someone had rifled through her belongings; I feel that way letting a friend use my laptop.

I was also framing her world on my terms, which are skewed by my compulsion to affirm the person I think I am. My documentation had an ulterior motive: my phone was a mechanism that could place me at a distance from any shared moment, turn it instantly into a minor spectacle for parties not present. I told myself this was a show of affection, but it didn't feel that way—it felt callous and performative, like placing my loved ones in scare quotes. I wanted to be present, to reaffiliate with my family; I knew the right thing was less an action than an orientation, but it's easy to skirt such imperatives. To reassume the role of your parent's child entails an internal rearrangement akin to shapeshifting, as easy to dread as to long for. Every time I go back I hope to stop resisting.

Instagram, or any platform for self-broadcast, materializes a tension in the overlap of any two lives: not only separateness of experience, but of language. You can't control what you mean to someone else, or how they'll share that meaning; no matter your fidelity to each other, you will make and remake yourselves at the other's expense, repackaging that closeness as much to dismantle as to express it. Intimacy is exposure, of course; it narrows the margin of self-creation and risks revealing you as something other than you mean to be. The instinct to self-expose is as obvious an antidote as it is a betrayal.

CONFESSIONS OF
A WHITE VAMPIRE

Jeremy Narby

In the 1980s I spent close to two years in the Peruvian Amazon living with Ashaninca people. My goal was to conduct an anthropological study of how indigenous Amazonian people used the rainforest. At first I paid little attention to what my Ashaninca hosts thought of me, because I had come to study them, and not the other way around. But I soon noticed that they too had an eye on me.

Most of the young people in the community in which I was living spoke Spanish on top of their indigenous mother tongue, and this allowed us to communicate freely. One day, several adolescents and young adults were asking me questions about where I came from, "What's it like in your land?" and "Where is your land?" In response, I spoke of a round planet on which we all lived. This led to some puzzled looks, so I began telling them what I knew about the movement of planets. Improvising with a lemon and a grapefruit, I mimed the rotation of the earth around the sun. Then I indicated a point on the lemon, saying, "This is Switzerland, where I live," and another point on the other side of the lemon to situate the Peruvian Amazon, saying, "And we are here." The young people listened to this demonstration in silence. When I was finished, they continued staring at me without saying any-thing.

Over the following months, I came to understand that the Ashaninca community had a different point of view on the matter. For them, the place I came from was not situated on the other side of a sphere on which we all lived, much less on the other side of a lemon. My world was situated *below* theirs. In their view, white people (*virakocha* in Ashaninca, *gringo* in Spanish) lived in an underground world—hence our pale skins—and accessed the Ashaninca's territory by passing through lakes. We lived in towns filled with sophisticated technologies, and we occasionally came up to the Ashaninca's world to capture their women and children and extract the fat from their bodies, which we turned into a fine oil that we used to run our machines and the motors of our airplanes.

I came to realize that many of the Ashaninca people I was living with considered me a potential *pishtako*—or "white vampire," who kills to extract human fat. I found it disturb-ing to think that people could see me this way. But over the months I began to think that the *pishtako* concept was in fact an appropriate metaphor for the historical behaviour of Westerners in the Amazon, who have long acted as a sort of vampire, extracting natural and human resources. In the six-teenth century, the first conquistadors destroyed and killed so they could return home with gold. Since then, the pattern has remained the same—Westerners have come to extract rubber, oil, wood, and minerals, often at the cost of human life.

From the Ashaninca point of view, I was undeniably a gringo: white. But beyond the colour of my skin, I also had blue eyes, fair hair, and a beard. And it so happened that these characteristics were exactly those used to describe *pishta-kos* at the time. As far as my Ashaninca hosts were concerned, I certainly looked like a *pishtako*. So it seemed reasonable to think that I had come to extract something.

Several times during my stay in the community, different men took me aside and confided that they knew of nearby gold deposits they would be willing to show me. They said this as if to test my interest. I would reply with indifference to these propositions, much to my interlocutors' surprise. A gringo uninterested in gold? Was it possible?

People would regularly ask me questions about the world of gringos. One question in particular kept cropping up: why is it that gringos never have enough wealth? You can give them gold, but they'll only want more. Why? For the Ashaninca, gringos seemed obsessed by the accumulation of matter, objects, and technology. From an Amazonian perspective, material accumulation had never been very practical, given the heat and humidity of the environment. It seemed unnatural.

My Ashaninca companions were still fascinated by the objects I owned, and tirelessly asked questions about them: How did I make rubber boots with leather linings? A Swiss army knife? A portable tape recorder? I may have been a *pishtako*, but I owned fascinating merchandise nonetheless.

This fascination with the equipment of white people extends across various indigenous Amazonian groups. For example, the Piro people's word for white people means "owners of objects." The Yanomami call them "people of the merchandise." Davi Kopenawa, a Yanomami shaman, says this of the white people he's encountered:

> Their thought remains constantly attached to their merchandise. They make it relentlessly and always desire new goods. But they are probably not as intelligent as they think. I fear that this euphoria of merchandise will have no end and that they will entangle themselves with it to the point of chaos.

As a student living with the Ashaninca, I became accustomed to being seen as a *pishtako*, obsessed with extraction and self-enrichment. But I also resolved to try to prove them wrong, to extract nothing, and to try to be useful to them.

After living with the Ashaninca people for twenty-one months, I wrote my doctoral thesis and began working for a humanitarian organization active in the Peruvian Amazon. Over the last thirty years, I have had the opportunity to travel around the region and meet people from numerous different cultures: Shawi, Awajún, Kukama-Kukamiria, Matsigenka, and many others. I was surprised to find that all these people refer to *pishtakos*.

In 2002, while I was travelling with the Awajún people in the north of the Peruvian Amazon, we made a stop at an isolated house that belonged to a member of our party. The fellow's wife welcomed us in, but when she saw me, she went pale and started shaking because she thought I was a *pishtako*. Her fear was so intense that she couldn't bring herself to approach close enough to give me a manioc beer, which she was serving to all the other travellers in accordance with the principles of Awajún hospitality. Her husband reprimanded her and told her not to be afraid, and to serve me a beer like she had everyone else. He worked as a bilingual teacher, and we had known each other for some time. When we resumed our trek, he told me that his wife was not used to seeing white people, and that her fear was not ill will.

It was then I realized that hosting a gringo–*pishtako* was like receiving a visit from Count Dracula himself, with his white skin and blood-tinged teeth. I was a grim prospect.

I made an effort to consider the following question: Was I truly a *pishtako*? A white vampire, here in the Amazon to extract human fat? I was certainly a child of capitalism, materialism, and rationalism. My ancestors had participated in the development of global capitalism, the wheels of which had been greased by the ruthless exploitation of indigenous Amazonian people. What I'd read of the atrocities committed against indigenous Amazonian people during the rubber boom of the nineteenth and twentieth centuries was certainly gruesome. It was true that my culture was *pishtako*-like, and that therefore so was I, at least to a certain extent. The *pishtako* image became all the more disturbing because it was coherent.

As an anthropologist, I had extracted data from the Ashaninca while I was living with them, which I then turned into a doctoral dissertation for my personal benefit. And now, as I worked for a humanitarian organization that backed indigenous initiatives like land titling and bilingual education programmes, I felt relieved that I could partly atone for my past. Reciprocity, I realized, is an antidote to *pishtako*-hood. But I did not discourage Amazonians from seeing Westerners as *pishtakos*, because I had come to view the metaphor as essentially true.

Anthropologists who have studied *pishtako* stories consider them part of a tradition dating back to the first contact with Europeans towards the end of the sixteenth century. These stories have long been told by native peoples in Peru, both in the Andes and the Amazon. For Peruvian anthropologists Fernando Santos-Granero and Frederica Barclay, *pishtako* stories reflect "a fear of white people and their predatory powers." But they also note that these stories have evolved over time. Those circulating in the Peruvian Amazon in the 1980s, which I heard with my own ears, responded to the aggressive government policy of colonization and deforestation. In 2010, a new kind of *pishtako* story was circulating through the region: the white vampires had gone from being individuals extracting fat to flying gringos, equipped with metal wings, who killed young people to extract their eyes, hearts, and other organs, which they would send on to the United States, where they could be used as transplants for the elderly. These contemporary *pishtakos* no longer emerged from lakes, but from the sky. When they moved, they emitted multicoloured lights, and they always carried a small freezer where they stored the different organs extracted from their victims.

But there is also another type of extractor that has emerged over the last twenty years as a new generation of white people has descended on the Amazon in search of shamanic experiences and healing. That white people should be in search of healing does not surprise anyone. From the Amazonian perspective, it makes sense that the children of *pishtakos*, whose lives are saturated with objects, technology, and materialism, should seek healing and meaning from Amazonian healers.

What's different this time around is that the white people say they want to learn from Amazonians. They're not coming to extract gold, or body parts, but to learn. And they're even willing to pay for this knowledge. All this is new.

What, then, do indigenous Amazonians think of the Europeans and North Americans who come to the Amazon to drink ayahuasca? I put this question to Amazonian people working to defend Amazonian knowledge and culture who have no direct interest in the ayahuasca economy, or in the commerce of medicinal plants.

Never Tuesta Cerrón, the Awajún director of a training program for indigenous bilingual and intercultural teachers, told me he felt optimistic about the new visitors.

"I think it is good that the Europeans get to know the knowledge of indigenous peoples." He was pragmatic and open: gringos should feel welcome to learn about their knowledge, all they asked was that Westerners respect the proper procedures.

But he also insisted that this was merely his personal opinion, which he viewed as insufficient to address my query. So on his own initiative, he submitted the question to several indigenous elders who work for the programme he runs, and who had been elected by their people to teach their language and culture to young indigenous teachers in training.

The elders who responded insisted that there was a connection between, on the one hand, the plant and the land; and on the other, the plant and the people of the land, who know how to use it. One of the specialists even wondered whether aya-huasca would have the same effect if it were drunk (or grown) in other lands. Ayahuasca is profoundly embedded in their space and culture, and it was unclear to some of them whether white people—who might or might not live in an underground world, with different rules and practices—would be able to use ayahuasca in the same way. What ayahuasca was in one world, they said, might not be what it was in another.

The elders believe that white people who drink ayahuasca outside its natural environment contribute to "breaking its strength" and "weakening the maestros"—the maestros being the shamans who prepare and administer the brew. White people are again seen as extracting vitality from the land, lay-ing down another strand in the evolution of pishtako stories.

"They already stole everything we had," one of the special-ists put it, while asking why Westerners must now take aya-huasca, too. Another suspected that what white people really want is to identify and steal the "essence" of ayahuasca, and with it the "spiritual force" of indigenous peoples.

I think there is a deep truth in the *pishtako* concept. Most Westerners, even well-meaning ones, end up in vampire-like relationships with Amazonians. Most often this is due to the power imbalance between the two sides. The problem is that Westerners stand to extract considerably more value from the encounter than the locals.

My life was certainly changed by living with Ashaninca people, much more so than the other way around. And West-ern ayahuasca drinkers often claim that their time in the Amazon changed their lives. But what do the indigenous peo-ple who attend to them get out of it? Perhaps some small form of payment, but nothing life-changing.

Undoing this imbalance, and making our relationship with Amazonian people more reciprocal, is the work of a lifetime.

MERITOCRACY AND ITS DISCONTENTS

James Brooke-Smith

What do Justin Trudeau, Donald Trump, Elon Musk, and Mark Zuckerberg have in common, other than being powerful white men? They have all made public statements defending their hiring choices on grounds of meritocracy. In 2017 Trump claimed his overwhelmingly white and male cabinet was based entirely upon talent. Trudeau recently defended the appointment of six federal judges in New Brunswick with close ties to the Liberal party as "merit-based." Musk has repeatedly cast his workforce, which is comprised of 28 percent women and in which a mere 11 percent of leadership roles are held by women, as a meritocracy. And Zuckerberg, whose company has been at the centre of an ongoing debate about diversity in Silicon Valley, has referred to Facebook's "hacker way" as "extremely open and meritocratic."

Trudeau might count himself unlucky to be included in such company, as his decision to have a fifty-fifty gender split in his cabinet was welcomed by many progressives as a step towards redressing centuries of gender discrimination in Canadian politics. But, as the above statements demonstrate, the ideal of context-blind meritocracy continues to appeal across the political spectrum. To those on the left, meritocracy guards against the inequities of inherited wealth and unearned privilege; to those on the right, it allows for the freedom of the individual to express his talents and achieve her proper level in society. For many, meritocracy has come to seem like the natural way to organize things. It's a no-brainer.

But what we seem to have forgotten is that the term "meritocracy" was coined to demonstrate the ills that might stem from the too-zealous pursuit of intellectual merit. In spite of its Greek etymology, meritocracy is not an ancient political concept, like aristocracy and democracy, but was introduced by Michael Young, a British sociologist and author of the Labour Party's transformative 1945 election manifesto, which laid the foundations of the post-war welfare state. His 1958 book, *The Rise of the Meritocracy*, is framed as a history dissertation written in 2033. It charts the emergence, over the course of the second half of the twentieth century, of a pure meritocracy. In his blandly scientific tones, Young's future historian describes the tyranny of the genetically fortunate over the rest of society.

In a dystopian Britain, children undergo intelligence tests at the age of three, members of parliament are selected by IQ score, and citizens must carry their "National Intelligence Card" with them at all times. In place of the class system that was forged in the fires of the Industrial Revolution, pure meritocracy apportions wealth and status via the scientific measurement of intelligence and effort: $IQ + E = M$. The result is a highly stratified society that, due to its grounding in empirical social science, is immune to political critique. The ruling class of scientists and politicians is unassailable in its intellectual excellence. The lower class of manual workers and servants is locked out of the high-tech economy by virtue of its proven intellectual deficiencies. As the historian blithely puts it, "Equality of opportunity meant equality of opportunity to be unequal."

If you strip away the science-fiction trappings, much of what Young says is prophetic of our world today. Of course, we do not live in a pure meritocracy, as Trump's cabinet picks, the Liberal's court appointments, and the workplace demographics of Silicon Valley make amply clear. Access to positional goods such as excellent schools, tutoring services, free time, and cultural capital skews along class and racial lines; the gateways to elite institutions are often narrowed by unconscious biases. Yet even if the playing field is not perfectly even, we all at some level adopt the ethos of competitive individualism that meritocracy entails, and many of us fall prey to the sense of entitlement that merit-based success can encourage. Sitting in my university office, have I not thought to myself, in the fleeting moments between student conferences and department meetings, "I worked hard to get here. I'm good at my job. I deserve what I have"? And does this not imply, as its unspoken corollary, that the people who serve me lunch in the food court or fix the elevator in my building deserve the considerably less that they have? This was the nub of Young's critique of meritocracy: that it undermines social solidarity.

But it is not just leftist academics like Michael Young who distrust meritocracy. As it turns out, some of the most prominent beneficiaries of contemporary American meritocracy distrust the effects of the system when it applies to their own children. This past March, the FBI disclosed the results of its "Operation Varsity Blues" investigation, which focused on William Rick Singer, a corrupt admissions consultant. In exchange for between $25,000 and $550,000, Singer would procure fake test scores, medical certificates, and sports records in order to help wealthy but undeserving children gain access to some of America's most prestigious colleges and universities. He drew on a network of corrupt officials: educational psychologists who wrote fraudulent medical notes granting students extra time on standardized tests; academic high flyers who took those tests on behalf of no-hoper candidates in "friendly" test centres; admissions officers who turned a blind eye to fake documents; coaches who reserved spaces on varsity teams for clearly incapable students. Thus far, fifty people have been indicted on charges of mail fraud, honest services mail fraud, and money laundering. Singer could face up to sixty-five years in prison.

The scandal abounds with juicy details and comic touches. The TV rights to an upcoming book on the affair have already been sold, and one can only hope that the mini-series will be given the full Bonfire of the Vanities–style satirical treatment. Most obviously, there's the celebrity angle. Two of the parents charged in the conspiracy are Lori Loughlin and Felicity Huffman, prominent Hollywood liberals. Loughlin and her partner, the fashion designer Mossimo Giannulli, paid $500,000 to get their daughter, Olivia Jade, admitted to the University of Southern California as a member of the rowing team. They succeeded in spite of the fact that Olivia Jade spent most of her high school years maintaining a popular Instagram account and marketing hair-care products, rather than bulking up on protein shakes and improving her oarsmanship. But even without the celebrity angle, the gap between the protagonists' slick self-confidence and their evident alienation from moral norms of fairness and honesty is rife with comic potential. John B Wilson, CEO of a private equity and real estate company, paid for his son's fraudulent entry to USC as an elite water polo player via his company expense account as a "consultancy" fee. Almost all of the payments were registered as charitable donations, and hence were tax deductible. That's elite-level fraud: fraud squared.

Most of the parents named in the FBI indictments come from what you might call the American petit-millionaire class, the ranks of real estate developers, media executives, investment managers, and corporate lawyers, who are not quite rich enough to afford the $10 million donation required for legacy admissions at elite schools but can still afford to pay as much as ten times the national average annual income to cheat their way in. It is all too easy to imagine these parents applying the same moral flexibility to their professional lives. The FBI investigation began when Morrie Tobin, a suspect in an unrelated securities fraud case, sought to curry favour with the Bureau by divulging information about his acquaintance with a corrupt admissions counsellor. In this case, the worlds of financial fraud and admissions fraud overlapped. But there is also a wider affinity between the two crimes. Both stem from the moral flexibility that can arise when the meritocratic ideal of individual success is pursued with excessive vigour. Operation Varsity Blues was the American higher education system's Enron moment, Lance Armstrong moment, and Russiagate moment rolled into one.

Surely the same thing couldn't happen here in Canada? Well, yes and no. The impetus to fraud stems from the highly stratified nature of the American higher education system, where a small number of elite colleges act as gateways to the upper reaches of the job market. These elite schools—mainly Ivy League and wealthy private institutions—maintain their status not only through expensive tuition and excellent facilities but also through the artificial conditions of scarcity they create. For the 2016–17 academic year, the acceptance rate at Yale was 6.3 percent, and the average annual fees at private US schools were $35,000 ($49,480 at Yale). At the University of Toronto, the acceptance rate was 69 percent, and the average annual fees at Canadian public universities were $6,838. There is also less distance to travel, in terms of prestige and public perception, between different institutions in the Canadian system. The distance between, say, the University of Toronto and the University of New Brunswick is significantly less than that between Yale and Arizona State University. One of the many comic moments in the FBI's Operation Varsity Blues report comes when Giannulli drops the A-Bomb in an email to Singer: "I want to fully understand the game plan ... as it relates to ... getting [Olivia Jade] into a school other than

ASU." This is a world in which parents are prepared to risk prison time and pay hundreds of thousands of dollars in order to avoid sending their children to a mid-ranking state school.

While the Canadian system is flatter and broader than the American one, its playing field is hardly a level one and is by no means immune to cheating. Huffman, Loughlin, and the rest of the Varsity Blues crew have been described as the ultimate "snowplow parents," who will go to any lengths to clear obstacles from their children's paths. Canadian parents might not bribe their kids' way into university, but many do pay for private schools, tutoring services, and enrichment activities to bolster their precious darlings' CVs and ensure their competitive advantage in life. I suspect that a number of students in my own department have at least some of their assignments written by their parents or hired help. Canadian academia is rife with essay-writing services, exam-cheating scams, and plagiarism. Reliable statistics are hard to come by, but a 2012–14 study found that 53 percent of 15,000 Canadian students surveyed admitted to cheating. In interviews, many expressed a blasé cynicism about academic fraud: this is how the system works; everyone else is doing it; you've got to get ahead at all costs. The amoral spirit of competitive individualism knows no borders.

Given these conditions, it makes sense to advocate for greater equality of opportunity and to work toward a more robustly meritocratic system, one that is immune to class privilege, racial inequality, and the pervasive culture of academic fraud. A true meritocracy would surely be a lot better than the imperfect one we currently have. But it also pays to remember Young's original aim in writing *The Rise of the Meritocracy*: his desire to highlight the older system of values that we sacrifice in adopting meritocratic competition as the primary criterion for social status. These may seem like antiquated concepts, but I'll name them anyway: solidarity, kinship, care, disinterest. In place of equality of opportunity—or "equality of opportunity to be unequal," as he put it—Young wanted to hold onto the ethical ideal of the equality of all human beings in the eyes of God. After all, where do our talents come from if not from God, fate, or genetic luck? Today's popular understanding of meritocracy encourages us to believe that we are our talents, and that we are thus entitled to the rewards that accrue from their exercise. Young insisted on the contrary principle: that everyone deserves equal status and respect, regardless of their high school GPA.

Meritocracy has the potential to alter the composition of social classes, but it retains the hierarchical structure of the class system itself. And with this hierarchical system comes an uneven distribution not only of financial wealth, but also of less easily quantifiable social goods such as self-respect, dignity, and recognition. In the 1970s, the sociologists Richard Sennett and Jonathan Cobb referred to this complex of ill feeling as the "hidden injuries of class." All too often, this psychic damage is unseen or poorly understood by those at the top. The hidden injuries of class remain obscure because those who suffer most are the least likely to be heard in the public square. Young extrapolated an extreme version of this situation in his future meritocracy, when his narrator notes:

> We cannot yet be sure just how much resentment the declassé person does feel. The very fact that he is stupid means that he is inarticulate, and the fact that he is inarticulate means that he cannot explain too clearly how he does feel.

From the meritocrat's vantage at the top of the system, wrapped in the blanket of his own preconceptions about how to speak and think well, he is unable fully to identify the underclass' resentment, let alone sympathize with it.

This is the seedbed of social conflict, both in Young's future meritocracy and in our own age of populist anti-elitism. You can hear echoes of Young's glib historian in Barack Obama's 2008 comments about rural white working-class voters clinging to their guns and their Bibles, and in Hilary Clinton's 2016 characterization of Trump voters as "a basket of deplorables." The disconnect between social classes is felt at the level of language and thought, as well as in economic and geographic terms. Indeed, many liberal voters struggle to grasp that it is precisely because Obama and Clinton speak in well-formed sentences, which obviously bear the imprint of their expensive educations, that they are so loathed by a certain segment of the electorate. It is into the linguistic and cognitive gaps between the elite and the underclass that mendacious opportunists like Trump and Farage insert themselves.

In the final sections of Young's book, we begin to see the meritocratic system crumbling under the weight of its own contradictions. By 2033, the original surge of social mobility that was unleashed with the introduction of meritocracy has given way to a new form of social immobility based on the inflexible code of the genome. Wealthy families have taken to kidnapping or buying gifted babies from poor families as replacements for their own unpromising young (a corollary, perhaps, of today's cheating and bribery scandals). The book closes with a wry editorial footnote, which informs the reader of the author's death during a riot at a mass demonstration at Peterloo Fields, in Manchester. Peterloo is a resonant name in British political history, the site of a parliamentary reform rally in 1819 that was violently suppressed by the military and memorialized in Shelley's poem "The Masque of Anarchy." The unfinished business of radical democracy is being taken up once more.

Young sets out an alternative to the winner-takes-all meritocracy through the Technicians' Party, a coalition of wives of government scientists, manual labourers, servants, and a handful of religious and intellectual eccentrics. The Party issues the Chelsea Manifesto, which envisages a classless society based on "the plurality of human values."

Meritocracies tend to privilege only a narrow part of the vast spectrum of human capabilities. Our academic system is good at testing abstract reasoning, scientific-technical knowledge, and rarefied forms of symbol manipulation, but has no measures for bravery, compassion, or intuition. According to the Chelsea Manifesto, in the just society "every human being would have equal opportunity, not to rise up in the world in the light of any mathematical measure, but to develop his own special capacities for leading a rich life." This would include equal recognition for skills in child-rearing, rose growing, and pottery, as for skills in management, computer science, and radio astronomy. Instead of grinding all differences into a single measure of academic merit (today's alphabet soup of IQ, SAT, GPA, and so on), the manifesto envisages a comprehensive system, available to all from cradle to grave, in which learning is decoupled from the job market, and all are free to pursue their interests and cultivate their talents. Freed from the exigencies of competition and status, everyone can pursue their vocation without reducing their chances of living a secure and esteemed life.

In the form of a radical manifesto in speculative fiction, this vision of the good society might seem impossibly utopian. But Young was no theoretical dreamer. In addition to drafting the 1945 Labour Party manifesto, he was the driving force behind the influential Consumers' Association, as well as Which?, its widely circulated magazine that used product reviews and technical research to empower consumers in the new post-war market economy. Young was also a founder of the Open University, Britain's largest higher-education institution, which to this day provides distance learning to predominantly mature students, often from under-privileged or non-traditional backgrounds.

Young was himself a product of social experimentation. He was educated not at an elite boarding school but at Dartington Hall, an experimental community founded on the agrarian socialist principles of the Bengali poet Rabindranath Tagore. His was a model of social entrepreneurship, preoccupied with the practical task of institution-building but always oriented towards the ideal of creating what he called a "commonwealth of opportunity" available to everyone rather than just a fortunate elite.

Young was part of the great wave of innovation that was unleashed in the decades after the Second World War, much of which drew upon the largesse of the welfare state and sought to promote broadly progressive and humanistic social values. In Britain and elsewhere, this took the form of child-centred and creative pedagogy in schools, expanded community and technical colleges, rising enrolments in higher education, and the creation of lifelong learning institutions such as the Open University and the University of the Third Age. In 1954, no less a figure than Winston Churchill expressed his support for a state-funded, non-utilitarian, lifelong educational system for all: "The appetite of adults to be shown the foundations and processes of thought will never be denied by a British administration cherishing the continuity of our Island life."

Rereading *The Rise of Meritocracy* prompts us to ask, Where did that generous vision go? Today's educational debate is a narrow, crabbed thing in comparison, more concerned with boosting GDP and equipping workers with skills for a rapidly changing job market than enabling all members of society to reflect on the "foundations and processes of thought." Insofar as we do hear radical voices in mainstream educational debate, they tend to emanate from Silicon Valley and the Californian educational technology industry, which is keen to convince schools and universities to replace face-to-face teaching with various kinds of online learning. Such "edu-tech" is often accompanied by a vague rhetoric of widening access and encouraging diversity.

In the age of massively open online courses, or MOOCS, and flipped classrooms, so the story goes, elite education will be available to everyone on the planet and no talent will go to waste. The gifted will rise, whether they are born in Palo Alto or Dar es Salaam. But the purveyors of online solutions are not really in the business of redressing the structural causes of inequality, nor of cultivating a "plurality of human values." The aim is to perfect meritocracy, not correct its blind spots.

We may be closest to the spirit of the Chelsea Manifesto—and to the kind of inclusive social innovation that Young practiced—when we're at the earliest stages of our current education system. In kindergarten, for example, learners are encouraged to explore the full range of their sensory, intellectual, and emotional faculties. Art, exploration, and imagination are to the fore. Caring, collaboration, and open-ended enquiry are not yet stifled by utilitarian concerns. Examinations and careers are distant prospects. Early childhood education is often the focus of our most generous visions of humanity and our most ambitious pedagogy. In recent years, this sense of idealism has driven a surge of interest in the Montessori method, the Finnish model, and the Forest School movement. Since 2016, the Ontario Ministry of Education has officially grounded full-day kindergarten programming in "play-based learning." We have the neurophysiological studies to prove that taxpayers' dollars are best spent on more time in the sandbox.

Why must we reserve our best ideals only for the earliest stages of the curriculum? Perhaps, instead of urging more meritocratic access to the upper reaches of our highly competitive and increasingly stratified society, we should in fact turn things on their head and extend access to the fruits of early childhood education much later in life—indeed, to every member of society. Kindergarten for all!

In the current climate, it's hard to imagine governments spending taxpayers' dollars on education for anything other than hard-nosed economic reasons. But this way of thinking can blind us to the social costs of elitism and the less easily quantifiable benefits of lifelong education. When we focus on the bottom line, we tend to ignore the relationship between greater participation in lifelong learning and economic "externalities" such as social cohesion, mental health, reduction of hours lost to illness, citizenship, and crime reduction, let alone intrinsic human goods such as happiness and intellectual growth.

In a 2017 paper in the *Journal of the British Academy*, John Bynner presented the results of his longitudinal study of the effects of lifelong learning on British age cohorts born in 1946, 1958, 1970, 1992, and 2000. Using statistical data on over 16,000 individuals from each cohort, Bynner demonstrated that those individuals who enrolled in any sort of formal education in adulthood—whether they took classes in accountancy or flower arranging, hairdressing or life drawing—displayed a decreased likelihood that they would drink or smoke, became less susceptible to depression, had increased rates of racial tolerance and political engagement, and had decreased tendencies towards political cynicism and authoritarianism. Lifelong learning, it would seem, is good for the economy, good for the individual, and, crucially, good for society as a whole. You might even say that, in contrast to more meritocratic competition in the school and university systems, it is one of the best tools we have for strengthening the collective in our uniquely atomized age. Wouldn't it be great if we could all go back to school this September?

OFF BALANCE

Jenny Ferguson

The First Thing

Warm, then searing. Those screaming nerves, the signal your brain sends to your body: take your fingers off the fucking stovetop. As you now know, it's hot.

The signal, your brain sends it. But it always arrives too late to stop the burn.

The scarred insides of my wrist act as proof of this. After pulling pizzas out of a hot oven, for years, I should know better, know these warnings, listen to them. Instead, I brush the shame away like a phantom itch, remind myself that I'm in my thirties and living at home for a year, and my life is pretty much the norm these days: too much schooling, under-employed but rocking the side-hustles, chronically single.

Like all other online purchases, my frantic search for a coupon code (single gentlemen readers between twenty-eight and thirty-seven years of age: I'm thrifty) is followed by held breath as I wait to see if my pilfered code actually works.

It does.

I may be living at home. But that doesn't mean I can blow 20 percent more than I have to here when I'm not even sure I want to do this. No, strike that: I'm fairly sure I'm not going to like this.

It's a distinction worth nothing.

But I often feel this way at first.

I'm often right.

I knew living at home with my parents, in rural Nova Scotia, where unemployment is climbing (currently sitting at 10.5 percent), where I have no hope of working in my field, where I have very little hope of developing a social life, where I'm going to have to live with my parents (more on this later), where my old car won't cut it on the poorly kept mountain roads (potholes almost as bad as Montreal—and that's saying something), I knew I wouldn't like this.

Three months and a bit into the experience, I'm right.

Okay, if we're being technical, I've lived in rural Nova Scotia less than that. Ten days after we committed my mother, I ran away to Eastern Europe to eat street food, among other things.

I'll get to my mother later.

First, I need to put my face online.

Sitting in front of my laptop, in the unfinished basement bedroom my parents have decided belongs to me, I'm calm now. I've also successfully managed to find my credit card (the one that has credit), and inserted the numbers into the field without backing out (this time).

I click the button. I pay the man.

My headline to lure the men: Over-educated and a little bored. We can only fix one of these things.

Like that Lincoln Town Car did when I was eleven, it hits me: I'm now paying money to look at men. I'm sure, shame hot, fingers burning like the element is on, brain firing off signals, I've make a mistake.

The Second Thing

A "member" for less than ten minutes and already I get the feeling I'll be axe-murdered before my subscription expires. And though I'm fairly certain that doesn't happen much, I Google my way to some statistic. The murder rate is actually decreasing in Nova Scotia (from 2.34 per 100,000 people in 2010 to 0.64 in 2014). That is, if numbers can be trusted, if a sick part of me isn't wondering where the numbers are for 2015? Where are the undoctored numbers? the numbers that account for my Indigenous sisters? The real numbers?

So while, according to the official books, the odds of my axe murder going down are fairly low in this province, it's the first thing I'm thinking when I notice one of the guys the internet thinks I might be attracted to requires the women he dates to be white.

I'll wait while you process that sentence.

And, okay, so you can't tell who I am from my exterior.

I like to smile with my mouth open. I have a facial piercing, and I like to buzz the left side of my head. But these exterior things might lead you astray, they might not be true, they might be temporary. The meaning you ascribe to the symbol may not hold.

I'm over-educated. I know this.

I also know attraction is complicated.

I know racism is real, is everywhere.

But stop the forward-seduction local single who only dates white people: you think you want me, but you really don't.

See, I'm the kind of Indigenous woman you might call "white-coded." But I haven't lied about it. I'm not trying to fool you, to pass. In fact, I'm attempting to understand all parts of myself better; to grow, to honour, and to support. Under race, I selected the "fill in the blank" option.

Say it with me: Métis.

Dear website, is your algorithm broken?

Dear website, have I confused you?

Dear website, do your users actually read? Did I assume people here would have some kind of proficiency with words?

Dear website, am I the flawed one?

Dear website, how many more of my matches will prefer I'm white?

Dear website, should I try to point out to these guys that there's something wrong, on a fundamental human level, one that turns me off, one that makes me angry, about their ideal world?

Dear website, should I write you a letter, you know, to point this out? to suggest you're part of the problem?

Dear website, am I over-thinking this?

Dear website...

And now, in the basement bedroom I'm starting to claim, even though I hate almost everything about it, I'm actively making plans to defend myself from the axe. Someone's axe.

I wonder, close to sleep, if my prized canoe paddle with the turtle painted on its fin will help at all in this upcoming showdown.

My Parents; *Before*

Every time we return here, my dad insists on going for a drive to look at the old high school. And when he says look, he means it. We sit in the dying van and stare.

East Kings looks exactly like it did back when my parents were enrolled here, my dad says, after a critical comment from the backseat. From me. To be honest, it appears to be in the process of being torn down. My dad ignores me and drives around back, where a teenager in a dark hoodie crouches behind some football equipment when he sees us slow, and eventually stop. He hides while my sister and I let my nephew, who is two, and *in* potty-training, pee in a plastic toilet in the trunk of the van.

I think he should pee in the parking lot. In the wild.

East Kings looks like that kind of place. And with that kid, wearing his baggy sweatshirt in the heat of August, hiding from us, it feels like that kind of place too.

Rewind to my parents' high school days. After all, that's why we're here, my nephew peeing, my dad and uncle sitting in the dying van, lost in their stories.

My parents didn't get along.

Mom was supposed to enforce the no-smoking rule. Instead, rebel-hearted, she lit up with a bunch of 1970s ragged teenagers, alerting everyone when one of her bosses appeared. All coins have two sides. If my mom's a coin, she's a poorly matched one. She's a complicated one. She's probably not a coin at all.

Dad, on the other hand, was tall enough to play on the basketball team, but all reports suggest he was never cool enough to properly belong. If this metaphor is working, maybe dad's a complicated coin too.

But my dad, the nerdy basketball player, was more into stamps than coins. And stamps do have two sides. But one of them is that bitter glue you need to wet, typically with the part of yourself that experiences the world through taste.

Maybe my parents are stamps. Maybe we're all stamps. This complicated, beautiful thing, perfectly clipped along the edges, but always bitter too.

It took graduating high school, and relocating halfway across the continent before my parents became an item.

High school. It's an ugly time. I weighed thirty pounds more than I do today; I wore sweatshirts (hey boy, teenage-me would have hidden too) because I thought they helped me conceal something fundamentally wrong about my body; I had homework, a part-time job; at one point I had three part-time jobs; and, for one summer, I genuinely believed this see-through pink shirt I owned, layered with a different shade of pink underneath, matched my red bellbottom-revival pants.

I must be a stamp too, my bitter a bit stronger, sharper in high school.

I can't imagine any of my peers as husband material.

That's a lie: I can. But he's very married.

And that's the end of that story.

The Third Thing

The first guy to message me writes well, and asks questions, and tells me about himself, and we have things in common, only I can't seem to find him attractive. I try.

Saying no, it's a problem of mine.

The concept isn't the issue.

I'm pretty comfortable telling you what I won't eat (meat/fish), what I have no interest in doing (skydiving), what I refuse to read any more of than I already have (*Fifty Shades of Grey*), what I won't take in a relationship (abuse: mental, physical, verbal, or otherwise). But I suck at saying no to people.

People are resilient. They prove this to me every single day. To live in this world, we must be resilient.

Yet, still, I feel, in some deep part of the part of the thing that makes this body into this person, that saying no to people like this man, who has put himself out there with good intentions, is inherently cruel.

Is that why when I swallow the bitter stamp taste I'm so relieved he set me up to walk away easy?

After I clear my palate with a thin chocolate mint, another part of me, the sick part of me, wants to send him a message. *You're not in it to win it. Don't you realize you're the one crafting the escape door—the one that leads away from you—that you're holding it open? No one should be that much of a fucking gentleman.*

I don't send that email.

Instead, I take his exit, pretending that yes, I believe it's possible to find someone to date—someone who wants to date me back—in a town of three thousand people, especially considering that Nova Scotia's home primarily to kids who are still legally required to attend school and to retirees like my parents.

Are you looking to date locally? a man living forty-five minutes away asks.

I take that exit like it's a MapQuest driving direction, and I'm gone.

The Fourth Thing

Rating men throws my (totally undiagnosed) anxiety (disorder?) into fifth gear. Send me into a suburban grocery store during canning season and I will battle it out with Italian *nonnas* to secure the best tomatoes in the market (okay, I lied again: the *nonnas* are way mor e aggressive than I am), but ask me to choose between a little green arrow or a little red one when those arrows are connected to people, and I'm a mess.

On bad days this makes me think I'm not cut out for the dating world's online evolution.

There are no good days.

My Mother; *Before*

There are no good days.

Dad keeps telling me (when we're sure she isn't listening in on another handset) that she has good days and bad ones, like they're divided out evenly and I keep calling on the little red days.

I wonder if the little green ones are the days she texts me at ten p.m.—midnight her time—asking when I'll be home.

She doesn't mean for Christmas, but for the night.

Like, in her mind, I live with her, I don't live 2,234 miles away.

I wonder if to my father these are the little green days because he's drunk or asleep when she sends me emails telling me my father is divorcing her secretly.

I wonder if these are the little green days to my father because he needs her days to be divided into little green ones and little red ones.

I wonder this long before she's disappearing for hours, little red days on end. I wonder this long before her delusions shift course, long before, in the world she's living in, my father is trying to kill her and I am helping him.

The Fifth Thing

His profile says, *Curvy. Yum.* and he is the owner of a really interesting chin. Square. Present. Real.

He messages me, using far too many emojis for my personal taste, but that's a really silly reason to stop talking to someone, right? When otherwise he's done nothing wrong? When emojis aren't really evidence that he's a flawed person, Donald Trump-style, at his core?

So I press on. Calmly. One message a day. Maybe one every two days.

(This reticence probably doomed us from the start. But over-educated does not mean smart. If I were smart I'd be a bored-but-well-paid government employee rocking my high school French and priority-hire status, and not under-employed, living in a rent-free situation.)

In his next message, he admits he's Pakistani and says, "I hope that won't be a problem for you (winky face)."

My snarky answer: "One of my best friends is Indian. I hope that won't be a problem for you."

It wasn't.

During our correspondence, I refuse to use emojis at all. A small part of me wonders if I'm emotionally okay enough for this if those too-bright, too-fake faces, expressing too-clear an emotion, are pissing me off to the point where I've started a silent protest, one I'm hoping he'll notice?

When I should be brainstorming how to flirt-not-flirt without crutches. Instead, I list the things I could have spent my money on: a third of a bag of dog food, a half bag of cat food, three-almost-four veggie-burger combos, two paperbacks (everything is more expensive in Canada), one paperback and almost-two veggie-burger combos—if I skip the poutine (sad face).

That Night

The thing you remember best is the sound of teeth chattering. Your teeth. Your jawbones clenching, your body taking over, on auto-pilot, no longer listening, like a bad dog, one you're yelling at, telling it to stop fucking licking itself, but no matter how loud you get, no matter how you beg, the dog won't stop.

You're underdressed for after midnight in early June. You're underdressed for being locked out of the house. You're underdressed for flashing red and blue lights. You've only joked about prostitution, post-PhD. Really, it's not even funny. Neither is this.

When you crawled out of bed, you found whatever, the jean skirt from earlier, because you needed something more than underwear to face your mother. You didn't want to be naked for that.

Good instinct, but in terms of execution, your jeans would have been smarter. Your black leggings—the ones you live in all winter—smarter still. A bra, yeah, that would have helped.

You remember half sitting, half leaning against the dying van—the one your mother drove off in hours and hours ago to do you don't know what, somewhere in this really pretty valley surrounded by ocean. You can still smell that dying van burn, the one it makes when it's been driven long and hard. Teeth chattering, your cell phone, you can't believe you remembered to shove it in your pocket—you're not that kind of woman—it's dying too. In the red.

Your dad, he's the kind of man who gives you his jacket because he can tell you're cold.

Oh, and you're crying too. Can't stop, even after the tears refuse to flow, can't stop so the chattering of teeth replaces salt as you wait for the police.

My Mother; *Now*, 1

The medicine has one detrimental side effect, the doctor warns my father and me in a British-inflected accent. It manifests as obesity, or diabetes, or heart disease.

These days, my mother likes everything I post on Facebook, so much so that I feel I'm actively being watched. In between liking me, my sisters', and my nephew's posts, my mom shares those videos where a camera watches a pan, the splash of oil, the ground beef changing colour, the toss of garlic, peppers, a can of tomatoes, until, three minutes later, the food that lingers on your screen smells like it belongs to you. She shares these videos one after another, an obsession.

Since I moved in, I haven't made myself a meal or snack where she hasn't needed to take something—one blue corn chip—off my plate, no matter how late it is, no matter how close my meal presses against her last.

Yes, she's gained weight. But that's okay. The woman who thought her husband was trying to kill her, who refused plate after plate, who stopped eating anything she hadn't opened herself, that woman needed to.

That Night

The female RCMP constable who shares a last name with Canada's prime minister (yes, the hot one) asks if you told the doctor you're not safe at home with your mom. If the doctor releases your mom, you're not safe. It hasn't occurred to you that safety is about more than your body remaining whole.

This is after your mother is handcuffed and taken against her will to the hospital. This is after you manage to put on more appropriate clothing. This is after you warm yourself, learn to breathe again. After you convince your father, who seems more relaxed with his wife in police custody, who cracks another beer, who doesn't seem to have heard the police, who doesn't seem to want to go to the hospital, who does seem to want to climb into your car and visit his wife in a locked emergency room.

When you shake your head, indicating no, the constable says, "He never keeps these patients."

She says, "If he releases her, we'll have to bring her home."

It's hard to trust the police, to trust doctors, when everything's gone mad-world, upside-down. In a private waiting room, you wonder how you'll ever forget this night, how hard you'll have to try to forget.

My Mother; *Now*, 2

The other side effect, well, maybe it's not a side effect. Maybe the medicine does exactly what it's supposed to.

The drug my mom is legally forced to take—let's not talk about the fact that the ones legally forcing her are my dad and me (supported, if it helps, and it doesn't, not for me, by our entire extended family)—sort of empties her out, so that, when I'm feeling empty too, I've called her a zombie.

I taste my bitter side sticking against my throat and gag. What I've said, more than once, is unkind, but it's not entirely untrue.

Rebel-heart.

A woman who laughed. A lot.

Who was easily hurt.

Who didn't understand but always tried.

Who called cashiers "dear," and "doll," pet names I always felt were inappropriate to put upon strangers who are forced by their very jobs, that thing that feeds their kids, to be nice, even when my mother would reach out and touch them.

Who never stood in my way.

Who has always talked politics with me.

Who has always understood what it's like to be the sober one in a house of drunks.

Who has always understood what it's like to live with a beating heart stitched onto her sleeve, where anyone can crush it.

The woman I live with now, she's not my mother. I keep waiting for her to develop a taste for grey matter.

But the woman who would text me horrible things, who said things *that night* that you never expect to hear out of your mother's mouth, that woman wasn't my mom either.

And since she's made it this far out of her delusions, since the doctors never thought she would, since she's taking the medicine, since she's not fighting us (aggressively), since she isn't running away, since she's stopped texting me anything other than, *Goodnight, I love you*, since we've come this far, I want to cling to the stories my friends seem to now have about their brother-in-law's mother or their own (why is it always the mothers?) returning to normal. But over-educated as I am, I know normal is not possible, was never possible in the first place.

It's hard to hope for better.

Harder still to accept this is what is, what will be, what we have left.

The Sixth Thing

Grey and I have a lot in common, he says. Yes, he's also working on joining the over-educated. He also likes nachos. But unlike me, he has a full-time-with-benefits job, an ex-wife, and he doesn't look like he's in his early thirties.

In the classroom, he must never endure the scrutiny of a student asking him his age. Maybe it's the grey, or maybe it's because he's a man.

Of course, he doesn't use emojis to express himself. He's not that kind.

He lives in town.

When he tells me this, something clamps down hard.

Too damn close, dude. This is where I live, dude, I think, as if he's invaded something private, as if this isn't his town as well.

My Father; *Before*

He always had a temper.

But so do I.

I believe we all get angry, that irrepressible shaking of our core selves that changes the way our features lie on our bones. This is very scary to witness because we recognize its intensity in ourselves. Or we recognize how this anger has changed us. Anger is human. The only difference I see worth discussing is how we express it.

My dad, he slams his fist into drywall, once a steel door, and once not his fist, but a wrench, into the rear flank of his car. I suppose the car wasn't participating, that nut wasn't coming loose, those fucking ants wouldn't leave him alone, the sun hot, the car infuriating, his patience ticking away until the car—an inanimate object with no ability to cause anger in itself—got the brunt of the day. That is to say, when my dad's face shifts over his bones, he hurts the house, his car, and he hurts himself. Not other people.

He's the kind of man I admire for how he handles difficult situations, for how he handles his own flaws.

Once he told me that the last time he remembered being truly happy was when me and my sisters were little kids.

A lifetime ago.

That Night

You don't believe in God, or gods, or fate, or much at all. You believe in creativity, science, what humans can do, and above all, you believe in balance.

You believed in balance long before you knew that the Métis Nation represents itself with an infinity symbol, long before you knew that Michif, the language of the Métis, is composed out of French nouns and Cree verbs: two cultures connected as one, forever. Of course, you understand this, the power of symbols. But in your blue eyes, you still see that infinity symbol on a blue background, that flag, as a statement about balance. What it looks like, how you find it, how you keep it across generations.

Sitting in a canoe, you can lean one way, and you can lean away before, if the wind picks up and the waves rise on this lake, before you'll capsize.

Of course, you know how right your canoe.

But that knowledge doesn't make you crave balance, worship it, any less.

That night, you look at it like this, when you can look at it at all: so many things had to fall into the perfect balance (the right cop, whose own mother had a long history with hospitals, red and blue lights; the doctor leaning against his grain; your mother showing the right symptoms; your mother absconding from the hospital that night; your mother being found; your mother speaking to two other doctors the next morning) for you to commit your mother against her will to a locked psych ward.

When this is balance, your axis is broken, you're broken, balanced but broken. You're fluent in French, but know nothing of Cree. You're full of nouns, emptied of verbs.

My Father; *Now*; My Parents; *Now*

They play backgammon together most nights, sitting at the too-large formal dining table. If she laughs now, a rarity, she's usually laughing with him. He's happier than I can remember.

Before she got sick, I would have told you I was surprised they hadn't divorced. While she was untreated, driving wild who-knows-where, I expected my parents' love story would end in divorce. Even Mom, in her shifted world, imagined my father secretly filing papers—no matter how many times I explained that divorce can't happen in secret. Her signature mattered as much as his.

While she was hospitalized, I riffled through the room she kept locked, found every single paper she considered valuable—birth certificates, passports, drawings from my youth—and a form from a local lawyer's office to rewrite her will. I wondered if the lawyer's secretary took my mom seriously, or if she dismissed her. I wondered how far she could have gone before someone started asking questions. What do they say: of sound mind? I wondered how long my dad would be able to keep up, how long he'd cope, when he'd get a haircut, when he'd stop loving her.

On very bad days, I think I already have.

But no, this isn't that story. Somehow, now that she's on medication, they get along.

Maybe this is okay.

End stop. Full stop. Just stop.

Maybe this is their happily ever after.

The Seventh Thing

The town my parents retired in is absurdly cute. The kind of place where storefronts are chic, you can park for free downtown, where there are no stoplights anywhere, and where pedestrians have the right of way. There's a reason tourists flock here; why, as you drive along the main drag, you won't find a single proper hotel. Instead, it's B&Bs, restored Victorians, one after another in blues, yellows, classy reds.

You should visit.

Really.

We have apple orchards, and local cider, and local tomatoes on local pizza, and craft beer, and even, if you look up, eagles circling as they hunt.

I don't work for Wolfville Tourism. This place, it's easy to admire. Easy to imagine lives here are perfect when on crisp autumn days you can walk to the grocery store, pay without a line, and get your fair-trade, micro-roasted coffee.

All this to set the scene, not to sell you a timeshare.

(Timeshares are so Florida.)

My parents and I are returning to town after grocery shopping at the Atlantic Superstore twenty minutes away. It's all but impossible to drive through town without stopping for at least one pedestrian—except, of course, when you're returning from the hospital at five in the morning.

Grey presses the button. Grey crosses the street. Or a Grey lookalike presses the button and crosses the street.

I don't think; I react, hide.

Later, safe at home, I try to understand why my first instinct when I spot a man in the wild is to run.

I compose a mental list:

I've stopped wearing makeup.

I haven't cut my hair in over a year. At first, laziness, or end-stage-PhD-ness was to blame. Later, the twenty-five dollars for a cheap cut was steep. At this point, let's be honest: I simply can't be bothered to care.

I'm losing weight without trying.

Not sleeping, not like a regular person. Sometimes it's Benadryl, sometimes it's something prescription. But most nights it's a book and purple earplugs and the hope that maybe tonight will be different. In the morning, almost always, because I live with a normal person, and a woman who, for the first time in her life (under medication), has become an early riser, I look like the deficient one. I am the deficient one.

Over the past six months I've lingered on the word suicide in the way I've lingered on other words: dissertation, missing and murdered Indigenous women, job hunt.

(Don't worry: I know this is a sign I'm in trouble. I know better. I have a dog, a cat, parents, sisters, nephews, friends, people who need me, who balance me.)

I've lingered over the word anti-depressant.

Honestly, I prefer books to people. The local library, housed in an old train station, is where I get my fix.

The American election season (a season that starts far too fucking early) is making me sick.

#BlackLivesMatter#NoDAPL#MMIW#WeNeedDiverse Books

These amply the things keeping me awake at night.

When everything's out of control, you're raging out of control, there's no balance, no solid ground, and you're hiding in a truck with tinted windows from a man who might be the man who messaged you online, you probably shouldn't be dating.

I realize how tired I am of shame, how much I want my forty-some dollars back, how much ending this online dating experiment will lift some of the weight, how I don't want to feel like I'm drowning anymore when I know damn well how to climb back into my canoe, how deeply I miss the taste of balance, the sweet, the salty, the sour, the savoury, and yes, the bitter too, these components of a resilient life.

The Post-Script

After the Grey incident, I quit the online dating subscription, and when the website tries to convince me to stay, I remain firm. When the website wants to know why, I leave the field blank.

In October, with my parents on vacation, I go to the doctor. I talk. He talks. I laugh. He laughs. He says the kindest thing: "You have some very real reasons to feel the way you do."

I leave with a prescription.

I swallow a pill.

That night, I dream in full sentences. That's it. One full sentence at a time.

It's strange and I can't tell if it's better or worse or if I look like I've slept at all, or if I care to keep feeling the side effects that lead to feeling better.

But I sign up for another online thing. This time, it's a language class: Conversational Cree. And I have a feeling I won't regret this at all, and maybe that needs to be good enough, for now.

FROM BERTH TO DEATH

Andrew Nikiforuk and *Amorina Kingdon*

US Navy soldiers lowered seven army coffins into the cold swell one by one. They said the names of the victims and a few words of solace. But they had other things to fret about as the *Leviathan*, queen of army transport ships, sped at 21-and-a-half knots on its way home to New Jersey—slowing down in U-boat territory was not an option.

The *Leviathan* was shuttling soldiers from the United States to Europe and had departed for its return voyage from France the previous day. It had left behind dozens more dead soldiers, none casualties of the war. They had died on the voyage over from North America, their war was with a deadlier foe: the greatest pandemic in modern history.

Ten days earlier, on September 29, 1918, the *Leviathan* had slipped its moorings in Hoboken, New Jersey, carrying over nine thousand army personnel bound for the killing fields of France. The most noteworthy passenger, however, was an influenza virus.

Many of the troops boarded with pounding headaches and sore throats. Some dropped listless on the dock before they reached the vessel. Ship doctors sent a few patients back to shore, but the war was more urgent than a coughing fit or a fever, and the crew set off as planned. Within twenty-four hours of leaving port, the virus had infected seven hundred troops and the sick bay was overflowing. Within a week, that number climbed to two thousand as blood, vomit, and sputum coated the decks.

Caregivers knew they had to separate the sick from the healthy, but on the *Leviathan* that proved impossible. The disease overwhelmed the bunk space. The *Leviathan* was a converted luxury liner designed to comfortably convey 6,800 souls, about twice the capacity of the *Titanic*. But the army had retrofitted the ship with stacked bunks and loaded it with nine thousand soldiers on top of the more than two thousand crew. The airborne flu traveled with ease around the crammed ship. Harried staff tended to the sick lying on the decks and in the hallways: flu victims burning with fever and drowning from fluid-filled lungs.

An official military report on the voyage described the scene: "Pools of blood from severe nasal hemorrhages of many patients were scattered throughout the compartments and the attendants were powerless to escape tracking through the mess, because of the narrow passages between the bunks."

The real horror of the outbreak aboard the *Leviathan*, though, was that it wasn't an isolated event. Around the world, the same scene was playing out among soldiers and civilians, from isolated islands to teeming metropolises, from North America to Auckland, New Zealand. A horrifying flu had hit eerily fast and hard, striking the healthiest of people.

The pandemic, known as the Spanish flu, hit hardest from October 1918 to March 1919. Today we know that particular flu strain was more awful than usual. But its deadliness was amplified by crowded conditions, the ravages of war, and a revolutionary invention in maritime technology—steamships.

Steamships more than halved sailing times, carried more passengers than sailing ships, and more efficiently conveyed pathogens from one shore to another. Steamships spread the

Spanish flu, carried in the lungs of sailors, soldiers, coal stokers, and civilians, to almost every corner of the world, infecting a third to half of the world's 1.9 billion people and killing more than fifty million in six months. The death toll may have reached as high as one hundred million over the course of the pandemic, but the chaos of the war and incomplete records cloud its true global impact. At the very least, influenza killed five times as many people as the First World War.

Since 1918, globalization has further shrunk the world. Today's military carriers and cruise ships, not to mention airports and jetliners, struggle with their share of diseases like norovirus, but the flu remains a major candidate for a global pandemic. And in any pandemic, a critical variable is how fast the disease moves. As we grapple with the questions of if and how to monitor for diseases in today's accelerated transportation networks—speed kills, after all—what can we learn from the dark duet of the Spanish flu and steamships?

The Industrial Revolution radically altered life in the West. Nations focused on building factories, roads, railways, and cities. By the mid-nineteenth century, everything and everyone moved faster and went farther. Railroads linked the once-remote edges of broad continents. But perhaps no technology affected the pace of living more than the coal-fired steamship. Replacing slow and often inefficient sails at sea, the steamship methodically contracted the world.

When the first steamships lumbered onto the waves in 1820, they were slow and clunky—not much better than sailing ships, which at the time took nearly a year to circumnavigate the globe. By the 1890s, steamships had reduced the journey to one hundred days, and, since they were now cheaper to build and easier to run than sailing ships, they proliferated and soon dominated the seas. Plus, they could handle more cargo. Within decades, the volume of goods traded globally increased by a factor of six.

Improvements to steamships, such as lighter hulls and more powerful boilers, coupled with infrastructure projects like the first undersea telegraph cables and the Suez Canal, in 1866 and 1869 respectively, made communication and trade between Asia and Europe effortless. British marine economist Martin Stopford says this connection had social impacts, including the consolidation of European empires. "The empires created a culture of continuous global travel," Stopford says. This drastically increased the movement of people, military and civilian.

Epidemics have always followed maritime routes: the Black Death entered Europe via Italian ports, Captain Cook and other Europeans' voyages introduced new and horrific venereal diseases to the South Pacific, and Irish emigrants fleeing the potato famine by ship were infamously riddled with typhus. Disease spread depends on variables such as infection rate, sanitation, contagion period, and available vectors, such as rats and fleas. Ships have all the right variables. Cram people close together, a few of them sick, move them around quickly so they infect new people, and watch the magic unfold. It's basic math.

From its inception, the steamship warped disease exchanges. Cholera, previously considered an Asiatic disease that only occasionally poked its nose into Europe, exploded along Mediterranean steamship trade routes in 1865. One astonished British doctor noted that the disease, while being no more deadly than previous outbreaks, had spread as far in six months as previous outbreaks had in two years. He wrote that "the unparalleled rapidity of progress finds no explanation in any peculiar virulence of the disease but solely . . . in the greater rapidity of traffic between different countries." This became the new norm: even if a country got word of a disease outbreak on the other side of the world, it had less time to prepare than it had in the past since the infected could be days instead of weeks away.

By the time the Spanish flu virus emerged, just over fifty years after that worrisome, speedy cholera, it found an even more developed transportation network connecting major cities around the world and growing networks in places such as the South Pacific that had never had consistent global transport links before. Moreover, at the start of the First World War in 1914, bigger and faster engines had reduced the journey time across the heavily travelled Atlantic from several weeks, in the early days of steam travel, to just five or six days.

Michael Worobey is an evolutionary biologist at the University of Arizona. He studies the evolution of flu viruses past and present. Before steamships, a flu could come on board a sailing ship making a transatlantic crossing but not survive disembarkation. "It could move through the whole ship's population and be gone by the time you get to the port four weeks later," he says. "The steamship essentially allowed you to have a person who was infected when they got on and infected when they got off." The virus never had a chance to burn out.

Still, amid the urgency of war, major medical authorities didn't regard the flu as enough of a reason to quarantine a ship or close a port. The seasonal nuisance killed the vulnerable— mostly infants and the elderly—leaving the healthy with, at most, unpleasant aches and pains. There was, however, a foreshadowing of flu's global potential in the steamship era during a Russian outbreak in 1890.

This outbreak was mild but spread fast. It reached the United States from Saint Petersburg in seventy days, and traversed the planet in just four months. One British account noted, for example, that in Singapore the disease arrived via mail ships from Britain and other ports to the west. The sick spread the flu to wharf workers, and from them the infection was passed from person to person. A 2010 study called the Russian pandemic the first to occur in a "highly connected world," one linked by trains and steamships.

The global aspect of the Russian and subsequent Spanish flu, Worobey says, was likely a result of steamships. "That was probably the first time in history where you could have, within in a matter of a couple weeks, flu viruses that could get to pretty much every corner of the world," he says.

The Russian flu killed around three hundred thousand (maybe more) people worldwide, which wasn't enough to create a public health stir. A British report on the outbreak called influenza "a disease not indeed very fatal." Even when Britain passed its Infectious Diseases (Notification) Act in 1889, influenza was left off the list of a dozen or so culprits: only the traditional baddies like typhus, scarlet fever, and smallpox made the grade, and though there was some talk of adding influenza to the list in the 1890s, it never happened. The United States has required overseas consuls to report certain diseases since 1878, and within its own borders since 1893, but never flu.

Then came the First World War and a virus that suddenly mutated from seasonal nuisance to serial killer. In some cases, individuals died within hours of infection; in some small villages, particularly Indigenous communities in North America, most inhabitants succumbed. Nobody guessed the virus could do that, and the reasons why would remain murky for nearly a century.

Scientists have long speculated about what made the 1918 virus so lethal. "It was never clear why it was so virulent," explains Darwyn Kobasa, a research scientist in the Zoonotic Diseases and Special Pathogens Division of Canada's Public Health Agency. Kobasa has spent more than a decade studying the Spanish flu strain in a secure lab in Winnipeg.

Kobasa was part of a medical team that replicated the virus in 2004 using samples obtained from three exhumed 1918 flu victims. Kobasa and his coworkers inserted two genes of the deadly virus into a mild flu virus in mice. Those two genes helped the mild virus bind to the mouse's cells. All flu viruses have those two genes, but the 1918 versions turned the mouse flu into an "ugly virulent virus in the mice," says Kobasa. Something about that version was turbocharged. The mice's immune systems went into overdrive, frantically responding to the pathogen, trying to eject it at any cost, wrecking tissues, burning energy, and even causing secondary infections in the process. The virus turned the immune system into a biological saboteur.

In 2007, Kobasa went further and introduced the replicated 1918 virus to macaque monkeys whose immune systems more closely resemble humans'. The virus provoked the same strong immune response. In an echo of the past, the primates' lungs filled with fluid and blood in an attempt to eradicate the pathogen. The virus kept on replicating even as the victims drowned. The blood and vomit that slicked the *Leviathan*'s deck wasn't the result of flu, it was the response of the soldiers' immune systems.

Intense crowding in ships and military camps may explain why the virus evolved into a killer, but the only thing everyone agrees on is that modern transportation was a huge factor in how quickly it spread, says Kobasa. "All of these changes in technology—the ability to move people everywhere and soldiers being housed in large camps where there was limited hygiene—all of these factors allowed the virus to spread so quickly."

With all this hectic movement, no one's sure where the whole thing started, but what is known is the pandemic had three waves. The second wave was responsible for the bulk of death and havoc, but the first arose almost half a year earlier, when steamships journeyed from the United States to Europe.

The most widely cited origin theory posits that the epidemic first erupted at a US Army training camp called Camp Funston in Kansas. In January 1918, local hog farmers near the camp developed flu symptoms and some eventually died of pneumonia. The flu sickened the hogs as well.

Illness plagued recruits at Camp Funston into March. From Kansas, these recruits were transported to eastern ports and shipped off to France. Somewhere amid the trenches and overcrowded military camps of Europe, the virus mutated into an even more deadly viral force. (Its moniker, the Spanish flu, arose because Spain, not being involved in the war, was the only country that didn't censor reports of the pandemic for fear it would impact the war.) It then boomeranged back to North America in a second devastating wave, causing the bulk of the deaths and mayhem on both sides of the ocean in fall 1918, during a time of unprecedented troop movement. This story of the Spanish flu's emergence has been the narrative for decades.

Worobey, however, thinks the flu may have made its debut closer to the trenches. Étaples, a base for front-line troops in northern France, offered perfect conditions for an outbreak with more than one hundred thousand people crowding the camp and its hospitals: ill soldiers with lungs compromised by deadly gas attacks and shipment after shipment of fresh troops.

Between December 1916 and March 1917, doctors at Étaples reported an unusual outbreak of influenza that attacked its victims so hard they turned blue with coughing. This was a whole year earlier than the flu at Camp Funston. Once the Spanish flu descended with surprising brutality in 1918, doctors who had treated the early cases in Étaples wondered if that halting first wave was a forewarning. They wrote to medical journal *The Lancet* describing the flu as "fundamentally the same condition as the influenza pneumonia of this present 1918 pandemic."

The doctors were witnessing the deadly second wave of the pandemic as it surfaced in three different military zones on three different continents. Crowded steamships connected all three centres of contagion.

In North America, Boston, Massachusetts became a flu hotspot in August 1918 after an outbreak at Camp Devens, outside the city. Designed for thirty-six thousand men, the military camp housed forty-five thousand. Navy personnel probably carried the virus to the Philadelphia Navy Yard, to Rhode Island, and by the steamship *Harold Walker* to New Orleans. From there, the virus spread westward and northward into one North American city after another.

In Europe, ports such as Brest in France had steamship connections across the ocean, and also across the English Channel, with the port of Plymouth, England, where the flu erupted as well. In August, the HMS *Mantua*, an armed merchant cruiser, left Plymouth and delivered the disease to what would become its third major epicenter, Africa.

Freetown, Sierra Leone, was a British colony and a major port on the continent's west coast where ships refuelled on their way to Asia. The *Mantua* arrived in Freetown with nearly two hundred delirious sailors; ten later died. The governor of the colony did nothing because influenza wasn't a reportable disease. Within two weeks, most of the city's population was bedridden, while a ship that had stopped to refuel in Freetown brought the virus all the way to Cape Town, South Africa.

But perhaps the greatest medical holocaust in history happened in the South Pacific islands. Soldiers returning to New Zealand from Europe brought the second wave with them, and it hit Auckland in October 1918, killing nine thousand people over a two-month period. The pandemic spread out unevenly, devastating some communities and leaving others unharmed. The hardest hit overall were military camps. The disease expanded out from New Zealand onboard the SS *Talune*.

The *Talune* carried one hundred and seventy-five passengers and a crew of fifty-six. Every month before and during the war, it sailed out of Auckland to deliver mail and freight on a regular route. It sailed first to Fiji, where it took on labourers for a two-week circuit through Samoa and Tonga before returning them to Fiji and then steaming back to Auckland.

But in late October 1918, the *Talune* steamed out of port for Fiji, carrying as many as five sick passengers. After a brief quarantine, the ship took on ninety Fijian labourers as always and headed off on its rounds.

The *Talune* docked on November 7, 1918 in Samoa. Ironically, the former colonizer—Germany—had quarantined ships routinely. But the current New Zealand occupiers weren't as punctilious, and at least half a dozen ill passengers walked ashore.

And then the dying began. "Every house was closed up with mats, and inside in the gloom the suffering of the inmates was pitiable to behold," wrote one witness. "Some lay writhing on the ground, some were covered with mats, sweltering in agony beneath the covering; others lay in silence." Over the following three months, Samoa suffered the greatest known proportional mortality of any state during the pandemic: 22 percent of the population died. The negligence in clearing the ship was so gross that New Zealand formally apologized to Samoa in 2002.

The dreadful voyage of the *Talune* also delivered the virus to Tonga, felling 8 percent of the population. In contrast, the nearby US-occupied colony of American Samoa, after hearing about the virus, imposed a strict quarantine on all ships and didn't record a single death from the 1918 influenza.

Ten days later, when the ship returned to Fiji, the ninety flu-ridden labourers disembarked to a crowded port: the war had ended on November 1 and celebrations had spilled out across the island. In the following weeks, the flu killed 5 to 6 percent of Fiji's 163,000 inhabitants.

Why didn't the authorities quarantine the *Talune* if they knew it had illness on board? Maybe ignorance was a factor, but so was the economy. The steamship's route and colonialism had connected these islands with a bustling global trade, and its timeline was driven by perishability. Two thirds of the islands' income came from exports such as sugar and fruit.

Any delay meant fresh food would rot and non-perishables would arrive late to New Zealand and Australia; money would be lost. Quarantine now meant a serious economic hit. Again, steamships forged connections that the flu exploited mercilessly.

After the tragedy in the South Pacific, the flu surged again in a third and final wave in the winter of 1919. It continued killing, albeit at a more modest rate, for a few more months. The final wave spilled into places that had, until that point, remained relatively unscathed, including California and Australia, before finally burning out. More than a year after its genesis, the 1918 pandemic came to an end, leaving only corpses, grief, and some cruelly taught lessons for future generations.

The 1918 pandemic taught us that disease moves quickly and that we should take the flu seriously before people start dying. The flu is not on the World Health Organization's reportable disease list: only yellow fever, plague, and cholera are. It's up to individual countries, states, provinces, or cities to make their own lists of reportable diseases. (The United States has infant-related influenza and Canada has lab-confirmed influenza on their respective lists.) Yet the flu remains one of the most common infectious diseases on the high seas, and still plagues military vessels, cargo ships, and cruise ships. When German researchers recently reviewed the medical logs of cargo ships, what they found was no surprise: flu outbreaks often sickened up to 41 percent of a ship's crew.

It's not just flu, of course. Cruise ships have become novel incubators for other infectious diseases, including the norovirus, an illness that leads to unforgettable bouts of explosive diarrhea and vomiting among passengers. The reason is, again, demonstrable with simple math. In the 1990s, the biggest cruise ship had a two thousand-passenger capacity, while newer ships now carry over six thousand, all in the name of economics. In the past decade, the number of annual cruise ship passengers grew from seven million tourists to twenty-two million.

A 2016 study in *Nature* declared the obvious about the health risks posed by these floating apartment buildings: "Long-term personal contact, complex population flows, a lack of medical care facilities, and defective infrastructure aboard most cruise ships is likely to result in the ship becoming an incubator for infectious diseases."

These vessels not only pack large numbers of people together, their passengers come from every corner of the globe. With each fresh batch of tourists exposed to infected crew or spaces, new microbial exchanges occur. Not surprisingly, cruise ships have hosted multiple outbreaks of flu over the past decade. During peak flu season in 2000, 37 percent of 836 passengers on a Sydney, Australia cruise ship came down with the flu. Several had to disembark at the ship's destination port of Nouméa, New Caledonia, before the return voyage, and two died.

That's worrisome considering cruise passengers' demographics. The average cruise passenger in 2016 was forty-six, and there are still plenty of fifty-five-plus cruises and senior discounts on major lines. So as a group, depending on the cruise, passengers can be more immunocompromised than the general population, just like gassed soldiers on the Western Front in 1918. Another lesson: be extra vigilant when it's crowded and when people are weak.

Cruise ships also mix passengers from the southern and northern hemispheres, and as a result can change the timing of seasonal flu outbreaks, which traditionally strike as the weather gets cold. One group of travellers likely brought a flu from the southern hemisphere all the way to Alaska and the Yukon in 1998. Over the summer, the virus may have infected more than thirty-three thousand people.

Another lesson: diseases are tenacious stowaways that exploit ships' broad travel itineraries and disembark in novel environments.

With more than a century of epidemiological experience, we should know by now how necessary it is to be cautious and vigilant—and how monitoring infectious diseases can avert disaster. But does the world have the necessary tools?

Worobey says there is no comprehensive surveillance system to catch new influenza outbreaks. The World Health Organization coordinates a network of national laboratories that can help detect the emergence of a new pathogen, but many parts of the world (such as sub-Saharan Africa) aren't sufficiently covered by this network. Further, surveillance is largely reactive, not proactive. National science labs research pathogen samples that come from hospitals or doctors' offices, only screening or sequencing a virus once lots of people fall sick. Take the 2015–16 outbreak of the Zika virus in the United States as an example: it reached Florida and Texas from Brazil via travellers who arrived on cruise ships and airplanes. Worobey says that with nothing in place to raise red flags when Zika first appeared, the virus was probably circulating in the western hemisphere for more than a year before anyone noticed it.

"We're always way behind the eight ball," he says of pandemics. "It doesn't have to be that way." When it comes to influenza, Worobey adds, public health labs often only check the antigen type to try to track what strains are going around when they could track the source and spread of influenza outbreaks more accurately by genetically sequencing the circulating viruses.

Worobey is a biologist now, but he once worked as a forest fire fighter in British Columbia. He says that in that industry, monitoring for fires is a constant thing. Weather is monitored. Every lightning strike is triangulated. Flights are sent out at the first sign of smoke. He says it would be easy, albeit costly upfront, to introduce a routine global monitoring system for influenza and other diseases, including reporting illnesses, sequencing virus samples, and tracking the first signs of trouble.

The world is more connected now than it was in 1918, and those connections are growing. Earlier this year, Qantas Airlines completed the world's longest flight—just over nineteen hours, New York to Sydney nonstop. In 2018, Royal Caribbean debuted the world's largest cruise ship, *Symphony of the Seas*, a 6,800-person capacity, twenty-two-restaurant behemoth.

We have solid road maps that show how pandemics happen. And they will happen: spotting those first signs of trouble would be good.

FOR THE LOVE
OF PRONGHORNS

Alanna Mitchell

One of the rare disagreements between my parents came early in their marriage. My dad, George Mitchell, a biologist, had shot a magnificent buck pronghorn, had had its head taxidermied, and then wanted to give him pride of place in my mother's elegant living room.

My mother, Constance Mitchell, a modern painter who carefully curates her surroundings, was horrified. Immune to Dad's protestations that this pronghorn was, as he wrote in his journal, a "museum-quality specimen," she banished the stuffed beast to the basement rec room where it promptly became a quizzical witness to our family life. It was so lifelike that it often seemed to me it was simply passing by and had thought to poke its head through the wall, keen to see what we were watching on television.

Dad was right about one thing. Pronghorns are majestic to begin with, but this fellow was something special: inky Y-shaped horns as thick as my wrist, square snout splotched with black, supersized dark eyes tipped with long lashes, a pair of white chevrons running down the buff of his throat. Even after decades on the wall, his ears were pricked so high I could almost feel him listening in on our conversations.

My dad, who died in June 2017 at ninety-one, loved that pronghorn. But not just that one. He loved the whole species *Antilocapra americana*. In his 1980 book, *The Pronghorn Antelope in Alberta*, my dad refers to his passion as an affair of the heart that never lost its fire. Maybe it was the lure of the unknown. The pronghorn was a scientific mystery when my dad was hired as the Alberta government's first game biologist in 1952 and began to study it.

Even the basics were obscure. At what age did pronghorns begin breeding? How many young did they have? What did they eat? How did they survive the winters? How many were there in Alberta and Saskatchewan, the very northernmost tip of its continent-wide range? How many had there been?

All unknown. But unless you knew this most elementary information, how could you predict whether they would stick around? He set about the messy, painstaking, life-consuming business of finding out.

The pronghorn's ancestor evolved in North America around twenty-five million years ago. Eventually, that ancestor, *Merycodus*, spawned a family of about a dozen species of hooved grazers whose size ranged from that of a jackrabbit to the lone, big survivor that became swift enough to race the hungry cheetahs and fearsome hyenas that then populated North America.

But while the cheetah, hyena, and all the other pronghorn relatives died out in North America—the pronghorn's closest genetic relative today is the giraffe—*Antilocapra americana* triumphed. And while it is the fastest land-runner in the western hemisphere, having been clocked in a sprint at 100 kilometres an hour, its unique gift is its ability to go the distance, both literally and metaphorically. It has an uncanny ability to convert the oxygen in its muscles into velocity, to keep up a car-level pace for ten minutes.

The pronghorn survived not only the climate stresses of the ice age, but also the arrival of humans, becoming the main grazer of the North American Great Plains. Its range exceeded even that of bison.

Theodore Roosevelt, twenty-sixth president of the United States, was fascinated with what he often called the pronghorn antelope, writing about its tremendous speed, sharp sight, and sweet meat. But he confessed himself baffled by its behaviour.

"Antelope possess a most morbid curiosity," he wrote in his 1885 book *Hunting Trips of a Ranchman*. "The appearance of any thing out of the way, or to which they are not accustomed, often seems to drive them nearly beside themselves with mingled fright and desire to know what it is, a combination of feelings that throws them into a perfect panic, during whose continuance they will at times seem utterly unable to take care of themselves."

All hunters had to do to attract a pronghorn in those days was wave a red handkerchief at it, Roosevelt writes. Fatally inquisitive, it would draw ever nearer, stamping and snorting, until it got within rifle range.

By the time my father was born in 1925, the pronghorn was near extinction. From a North American peak population of about thirty-five million a century earlier, the species was reduced to as few as thirteen thousand, says John Byers, a zoologist at the University of Idaho who has studied the animals for thirty-five years. That's a drop of 99.996 percent.

The reasons? Hunting, some of it to feed a trade exporting wild meat to Europe; the campaign to rid North America of wolves, grizzlies, and cougars, because when they were gone, the coyote reigned to feast on pronghorn fawns; plus the miserable cold and deep snow that plagued the beginning of the twentieth century.

And fences. Although pronghorns can jump—Byers has seen one jump over a human—they choose not to. They always think there's another way around. But as the Prairies became more settled, fences began to abound. Pronghorns, many of which migrate hundreds of kilometres a year seeking food, could no longer get through.

When my dad started studying them, their numbers had crept up thanks to a ban on the meat trade, but they were still in considerable peril.

I spent my childhood summers scanning the Prairies for them. My family would be driving along the Trans-Canada Highway from Regina, where my dad began teaching at the university in 1966, to the Pacific Ocean—"the coast," we called it. Pronghorns travel in herds, white bums flashing, legs seemingly too spindly to hold up their robust bodies, terribly alert.

Every time I saw them, I was overcome with wonder at their synchronized speed. I had no idea that they had once been so much more plentiful. And despite my dad's chops as an ecologist, I had no idea then that pronghorns are remnants of what was once a far richer dance of life on the Great Plains, including the extinct pronghorn kin and cheetahs and hyenas, but also dire wolves, giant short-faced bears, lions, jaguars, mastodons, woolly mammoths, and ground sloths, among many others.

"In the hurtling pronghorn, the vanished predators have left behind a heartrending spectacle," writes the journalist William Stolzenburg in his 2008 book *Where the Wild Things Were: Life, Death, and Ecological Wreckage in a Land of Vanishing Predators.* "Through the smoking displays of wild abandon runs a desperate spirit, resigned to racing pickup trucks in its eternal longing for cheetahs."

Biology was different when my dad was doing it. Nature's rules were there to be cracked like a code, to be parsed, catalogued and marvelled at, species by species. They were timeless certainties, revealed only if one were intrepid enough.

The fable of immutability has long been abandoned. Today's overriding scientific narrative is to figure out what the rules used to be and how they're changing. The great pulse of

carbon dioxide our species has been putting into the atmo-
sphere since the Industrial Revolution has pushed the planet's
chemistry to a place it hasn't been for tens of millions of years.
This has brought disruption to weather patterns, precipita-
tion, temperature norms, ice cover, and ocean acidity.

And to assess the effect those changes have on animals,
today's biologists prefer to observe them live, mainly in the
wild, often across ecosystems.

When my dad began studying them, focusing on a single
species was the norm. Killing was expected. Biologists were
collectors and archivists, preferably of enough samples to
compare. It was pretty crude stuff.

One of the scientific articles in my dad's slender collection
of published work describes how he and a co-author sifted
through 162 litre-sized samples of pronghorn stomach contents in a bid to see what the creatures liked to eat. The process
involved washing and sieving the partly fermented food—
cud, you would call it in a cow—then drying it on a towel and
identifying it. Silver sagebrush and pasture sagewort are the
pronghorn's preferred foods in southeastern Alberta, it turns
out.

Dad also tried to figure out how old a pronghorn was, a
basic piece of information that let him determine how many
adults compared to yearlings compared to newborns there
were in an area, and to try to work out what proportion of
each made for a healthy population.

The traditional way was to examine wear on the teeth.
Never one to take the easy route, my dad and his grad student Larry Kerwin would test the old method's accuracy by
counting the annual bands of cementum covering the root
of a pronghorn's tooth. Turned out this was far more accurate.

And this line from another article gets me: "The incisor teeth
used in this study were extracted from 190 mandibles obtained
by [George Mitchell] from mature pronghorn antelopes har-
vested in Alberta during the 1961–64 hunting seasons."

That's a lot of corpses from a lot of hunters. And there was a lot of work to do after he got the bodies. To get the incisors out cleanly, dad boiled every mandible in a pot of water for forty-five minutes. At some point in the process—post-skinning or post-boiling, I suppose—he would hang the jawbones on the back fence to dry. Once, my mother got a sniffy phone call from a neighbour who was having people for dinner: could the mandibles please be removed from the fence?

Little did the neighbour know what went on *inside* the house. It wasn't just the pronghorn head on the wall, or the bits and pieces of pronghorn carefully bagged but nauseatingly identifiable in the family freezer—"You never knew what you were going to find in there," my mother told me recently. "When I look back on it, I was terribly good natured"—but also the rows of pronghorn antelope fetuses suspended in formaldehyde in the Mason jars that lined my father's home office.

I used to look at them for hours, unable to stop thinking about the dead mothers they had come from, targeted because they were pregnant, wombs ripped open for their contents. They'd been collected in aid of another of my dad's findings—pronghorns conceive as many as nine young at a time, but only the two strongest survive. Further research by an American colleague of my dad's revealed that the most ambitious of those embryos get rid of their weaker siblings by stabbing them to death—the conniving twins practicing fratricide *in utero*. It was all positively mythic.

In my years as a science journalist, I've thought a lot about the theory that a scientist falls in love with a subject because it either embodies the scientist's personality or repudiates it.

For my dad, it was the former. Like the pronghorn, he had no siblings and few relatives. I think he felt like an outsider, born to a teenaged mother forced to marry his father because of him. They divorced when my dad was five, rare in Canada in 1930.

He was smart and graceful and devilishly hard to catch. I remember the tales he told of running feral in the Depression-era streets of Vancouver, stealing apples from the trees with impunity.

A survivor, certainly, and perhaps an unlikely one. His father got custody of him—a bigger scandal than the divorce—and his father's mother, blind from diabetes, tried to raise him. He used to talk about her attempts to sterilize needles in boiling water before injecting insulin, and about how she made him get coal from the half-cellar where the rats were almost as big as he was.

His saving grace, in a bizarre way, was the Second World War. He joined the Royal Canadian Air Force the minute he could and, with that binocular eyesight that could eventually spot a pronghorn at impossible distances, he trained for battle. The war ended before he got overseas, but along with his discharge, he got a ticket to university.

The first in his extended family of Scottish immigrants to attend university, he went on to get a PhD—on the pronghorn. To the end of her life, his mother lamented that he had never had a profession like her sister's son Doug, the fireman.

But I think it was the elegance of the pronghorn that really captured him. He longed for it. My mother said he brought home some young pronghorn and tried to raise them at the university, but couldn't get the milk formula right. They died of the scours.

Today, the pronghorn is hailed as one of North America's conservation success stories, a species brought back from the brink. Its global population is about 850,000. That makes it a species of "least concern" according to the International Union for Conservation of Nature, the organization that compiles the red list of threatened species.

Yet the biologists who study the pronghorn today are concerned about its future. A recent study of eighteen pronghorn communities at the bottom of the species' range in the south-western United States concluded that most of them will die out in that part of the country in a few decades as the climate changes. That was a phenomenon few scientists even imagined one hundred years ago.

Half the world's pronghorn population lives in Wyoming, because it alone in the Great Plains is lightly farmed. But Wyoming is likely to become less hospitable for pronghorns along with climate change.

Even now, almost all the ancient, narrow migration routes pronghorn once used in the Greater Yellowstone Ecosystem, which takes in part of Wyoming, are choked off by human activity, says Mark Hebblewhite, a wildlife biologist at the University of Montana in Missoula.

That matters, because animals that like to migrate but cannot are generally less healthy, he says. The ones that are still migrating are at a higher risk in general in a changing climate because they interact with more habitats and likely more human effects on those habitats. So, pronghorns will be hit with a double whammy.

Ultimately, climate change may mean more pronghorn come to graze in Canada as grasslands are pushed further north. Already they have been spotted near Edmonton, a more northerly address than they have had for years. Whether they will also be able to return south to escape ferocious winters is an open question.

And there are plentiful barriers within the vast Canadian landscapes the pronghorn craves. More farms, more ranches, more roads, and more fences mean less running room. Less ability to go the distance, if you will.

Hebblewhite wonders how climate change's weather extremes, combined with all those barriers, will affect the pronghorn. For example, in the bitterly snowy prairie winter of 2010/11, pronghorns died by the thousands because they pushed too far south in search of less snow and more food, crossing Montana's Fort Peck Reservoir. Once the reservoir melted in the spring, the pronghorn, poorer swimmers than jumpers, were stuck.

As much as 80 percent of the pronghorn population north of the Missouri River died that winter, including many that would have migrated to Canada, says Hebblewhite. To be sure, the population rebounded quickly and is now almost recovered.

And scientists, including those with the Wildlife Conservation Society in the US and the Alberta Fish and Game Association, are mounting programs aimed at modifying fences to allow pronghorns to wiggle underneath and preserve migration paths, yet it's believed that less than 5 percent of fences along pronghorn travel routes are modified, says Andrew Jakes, regional wildlife biologist for the National Wildlife Federation in Missoula, Montana.

Will any of my dad's pioneering work help the pronghorn survive its next set of challenges? Jakes says my dad's holistic work on the species "moved the needle forward" on its conservation in Saskatchewan. I know Dad had a lot more research about his beloved pronghorns and other Prairie creatures in notes that he never wrote up into scientific articles.

He tried. Long retired, his papers stacked in two tightly packed sheds in the backyard of our house in Regina, he would sit at the dining room table, surrounded by his data, trying to make enough sense of it to publish. Finally, he was diagnosed with dementia. My mother sold the big house and bought a condo for them on the coast.

My older sister and I flew out to help them clean out the sheds. He stood there, a frail figure with arthritic hands, his khakis impeccable, hair and moustache smartly trimmed, sifting through a single file folder for hours, trying to understand what his old notes meant. We finally took the whole lot to the university archives.

My mother shipped the pronghorn head to BC, although she never hung it up again. I'm not sure he noticed. By the time Mom threw a posh summer bash for her eightieth birth-day at a rented mansion near Victoria, things were starting to unravel. At one point my dad seemed a little lost. One of my cousins turned to him and said: "So, you were a biologist at the university, George!" My dad, who had lived and breathed biology for more than six decades, looked thoughtful for a moment and said: "Was I?"

The head did not survive Dad's move to the nursing home a few years later. My mother arranged for it to be shipped back to Regina, to the Royal Saskatchewan Museum, hoping that, still magnificent although missing one glass eye, it could go on display to honour my dad's work.

I checked recently. Alas, we couldn't provide accurate enough details of where and when my dad had shot it and, without that provenance, the head was useless. I'm told it was incinerated.

CONTRIBUTORS' BIOGRAPHIES

James Brooke-Smith is an associate professor of English Literature at the University of Ottawa and the author of *Gilded Youth: Privilege, Rebellion, and the British Public School* (Reaktion, 2019).

Larissa Diakiw is a writer, living and working in Toronto. She has written for *Hazlitt, Brick, The Walrus, Guts, Joyland,* won a silver 2019 National Magazine Award for her essay *Secrets Are a Captive Country,* and publishes Comics/Graphic Essays as Frankie No One.

Jenny Ferguson (she/her/hers or they/them) is Métis (on her father's side) and Canadian settler (on her mother's side), an activist, a feminist, an auntie, and an accomplice with a PhD. She believes writing and teaching are political acts. *Border Markers,* her collection of linked flash-fiction narratives, is available from NeWest Press. She teaches at Loyola Marymount University and in the Opt-Res MFA Program at the University of British Columbia.

Wayne Grady is a novelist, essayist, and translator. His novel *Emancipation Day* was longlisted for the Scotiabank Giller

Prize in 2013, and won the Amazon.ca First Novel Award. His third novel, *The Good Father*, will be published in 2021, as will his translation of Yara El-Ghadban's novel, *I Am Ariel Sharon*. With his wife, novelist Merilyn Simonds, he divides his time between Kingston, Ontario, and San Miguel de Allende, Mexico.

Alexandra Kimball is a writer and editor living in Toronto. Her essays and journalism appear regularly in national publications, including *The Walrus*, *Toronto Life*, *Globe and Mail*, and *Hazlitt*. Her first book, *The Seed: Infertility is a Feminist Issue* was published in April 2019 by Coach House Books.

Amorina Kingdon has been a staff writer and researcher at *Hakai Magazine* since 2015. She was awarded the prestigious National Magazine Awards Best New Magazine Writer gold medal in 2017. She has won several Digital Publishing Awards, and has been a finalist for the Jack Webster Award for Science, Technology, Health, and the Environment and the Knight-Risser Prize for Western Environmental Journalism. She also writes speculative and literary fiction, and her creative non-fiction was longlisted for the 2018 CBC Canada Writes Creative Non-Fiction prize. Amorina lives in Victoria, British Columbia.

Andy Lamey teaches philosophy at the University of California, San Diego, and is the author of *Duty and the Beast: Should We Eat Meat in the Name of Animal Rights?* (Cambridge University Press) and *Frontier Justice: The Global Refugee Crisis and What to Do about It* (Doubleday Canada).

Michael LaPointe has written for *The Atlantic*, the *New Yorker*, and the *Times Literary Supplement*, and writes a column for *The Paris Review*. His debut novel, *The Creep*, will be published by Random House Canada in 2021.

Benjamin Leszcz is a journalist, brand strategist and entrepreneur. A former partner of the design studio Whitman Emorson, Leszcz has contributed to *Conde Nast Traveler*, *Bon Appétit* and *Monocle*, and he has consulted with organizations including Google, Hermès and Hilton Hotels and Resorts.

Alanna Mitchell is an award-winning journalist, author, and playwright who lives in Toronto.

Alexandra Molotkow is a senior editor at *Real Life* and was a founding editor of *Hazlitt*. She has written for *The Believer*, *The New Republic*, *The Cut*, and the *New York Times Magazine* and was an arts columnist for the *Globe and Mail*.

Jeremy Narby is an anthropologist who spent several years living with the Ashaninca in the Peruvian Amazon. He has written several books about the systems of knowledge of Amazonian peoples, including *The Cosmic Serpent, DNA and the Origins of Knowledge*, and *Intelligence in Nature*.

Andrew Nikiforuk has been writing about natural history or the abuse of natural resources for more than four decades. His book, *Saboteurs*, won the Governor General's Award in 2002.

Michelle Orange is the author of *This Is Running for Your Life: Essays*, a New Yorker best book of 2013, and the forthcoming nonfiction book *Pure Flame* (2021). Her essays and criticism have appeared in *Harper's*, the *New Yorker*, *The Nation*, the *New York Times*, *Bookforum*, and many other publications. She is a columnist for the *Virginia Quarterly Review*.

Christina Sharpe is a writer and professor of Humanities at York University. She is the author of *Monstrous Intimacies: Making Post-Slavery Subjects* (2010) and *In the Wake: On*

Blackness and Being (2016). She is working on two monographs: *Ordinary Notes* and *Black. Still. Life.*

Carl Wilson is the Music Critic at Slate, and the author of *Let's Talk About Love: A Journey to the End of Taste* (Bloomsbury). He is a freelance writer, editor, teacher, and talker based in Toronto, where he's also helped run the Trampoline Hall Lecture Series since 2001.

PUBLICATIONS CONSULTED FOR THE 2020 EDITION

Arc Poetry Magazine, The Atlantic, Border Crossings, Brick: A Literary Journal, The Capilano Review, Canadian Geographic, Canadian Notes & Queries, Chatelaine, Corporate Knights, The Dalhousie Review, The Deep, Eighteen Bridges, Elle, EVENT, The Fiddlehead, filling Station, Geist, Globe and Mail, Grain, Granta, Hakai Magazine, Hamilton Arts & Letters, Hazlitt, Herizons, The Humber Literary Review, Literary Review of Canada, Maclean's, Maisonneuve, The Malahat Review, The Newfoundland Quarterly, The New Quarterly, Prairie Fire, PRISM international, The Puritan, Queen's Quarterly, Quillette, Real Life, Riddle Fence, Room, Slate, subTerrain, THIS Magazine, Vallum, Virginia Quarterly Review, The Walrus

ACKNOWLEDGEMENTS

"Meritocracy and Its Discontents" by James Brooke-Smith first appeared in *Literary Review of Canada*. Reprinted by permission of the author.

"The Disneyland of Death" by Larissa Diakiw first appeared in *Hazlitt*. Reprinted by permission of the author.

"Off Balance" by Jenny Ferguson first appeared in *Hamilton Arts & Letters*. Reprinted by permission of the author.

"Syncopes" by Wayne Grady first appeared in *Queen's Quarterly*. Reprinted by permission of the author.

"The Loneliness of Infertility" by Alexandra Kimball first appeared in *The Walrus*. From *The Seed: Infertility is a Feminist Issue* (Coach House Books, 2019). Reprinted by permission of the author and publisher.

"In the US Campus Speech Wars, Palestinian Advocacy Is a Blind Spot" by Andy Lamey first appeared in *Quillette*. Reprinted by permission of the author.

ACKNOWLEDGEMENTS

"The Unbearable Smugness of Walking" by Michael LaPointe. From *The Atlantic*. ©2019 The Atlantic Monthly Group, LLC. All rights reserved. Used under license.

"The Life-Changing Magic of Making Do" by Benjamin Leszcz first appeared in the *Globe and Mail*. Reprinted by permission of the author.

"For the Love of Pronghorns" by Alanna Mitchell first appeared in *Canadian Geographic*. Reprinted by permission of the author.

"Selfish Intimacy" by Alexandra Molotkow first appeared in *Real Life*. Reprinted by permission of the author.

"Confessions of a White Vampire" by Jeremy Narby first appeared in *Granta*. Reprinted by permission of the author.

"From Berth to Death" by Amorina Kingdon and Andrew Nikiforuk first appeared in *Hakai Magazine*. Reprinted by permission of the authors.

"How Free Is Too Free?" by Michelle Orange first appeared in *Virginia Quarterly Review*. Reprinted by permission of the author.

"Beauty is a Method" by Christina Sharpe first appeared in *e-flux*. Reprinted by permission of the author.

"It's Too Late to Cancel Michael Jackson" by Carl Wilson first appeared in *Slate*. Reprinted by permission of the author.